COLLECTIONS MADE EASY

*Fast, Efficient, Proven Techniques
to Get Cash From Your Customers*

By
Carol S. Frischer

CAREER PRESS

Franklin Lakes, NJ

COLLECTIONS MADE EASY
Cover design by Nunzio Carozza
Back cover photograph by Alan Ascher
Printed in the U.S.A. by Book-mart Press

To order this title, please call toll-free 1-800-CAREER-1 (NJ and Canada: 201-848-0310) to order using VISA or MasterCard, or for further information on books from Career Press.

The Career Press, Inc., 3 Tice Road, PO Box 687, Franklin Lakes, NJ 07417

Library of Congress Cataloging-in-Publication Data

Frischer, Carol S.
    Collections made easy : fast, efficient, proven techniques to get cash from your customers / by Carol S. Frischer.
        p. cm.
    Includes index.
    ISBN 1-56414-400-3
    1. Collecting of accounts—United States.   I. Title.
HG3752.7.U6F75   1999
656.8'8—dc21
                                                    98-50306
                                                        CIP

Dedicated to my dad,
Norton W. Ascher

Contents

Chapter 1

Introduction

Money makes the world go around. Like it or not, we have to face the fact that without money, we cannot survive. It is the very root of our existence. Money puts food on the table, clothes on our back, and heat in the house. Need I go on?

Very few people can deny that the more money we have, the easier life can be. And don't we all strive to lead easier lives?

Unfortunately, we do not live in a perfect world and the days of honesty and integrity at times seem like words from days gone by. Bankruptcy no longer carries the stigma it once did, and every day we see an increasing number of debtors taking advantage of the bankruptcy laws in order to relieve themselves of debts owed and promises made.

In order to stay in business today, it is imperative to have an impeccable system to track receivables. Receivables gone bad can, at best, result in lost revenue and, at worst, result in bankruptcy.

It is the intention of this author to get you on the road to an easier life by teaching you how to keep track of your receivables and have fun in the process. Perhaps you think I am overstating the "easier life" part. However, I have seen lucrative businesses go under because they let their receivables run amok, and by the time they realized it, creditors were at their door and banks were calling in their loans.

Before they knew it, attorneys were bombarding them with "deals" on how to file for bankruptcy. Regardless of what business you are in, it is certainly easier to deal with customers and clients than with creditors.

People usually cringe at the word "collections" and that is why they allow their own collections to get so far behind. How many times have you loaned money to friends and they did not pay it back? It becomes such an uncomfortable situation that most people would rather write it off than ask for it back. In business, clients are "friends" and millions of dollars are written off each year because it seems so hard to approach clients about money.

My career in collections began several years ago working for one of the largest public accounting firms in Los Angeles, California. At the time, the company had 10 partners and originally I was working for only one of them. This particular partner loved accounting but hated having to deal with clients about their past due receivables. I volunteered to help him with his collections and to make calls on his behalf, and that is how I got my start in collections. It was strictly by accident, but then, is there any other way to get into collections? Within just a few months, there was a noticeable difference between his receivables and the other partners' receivables, and they wanted to know what he was doing different to collect his money.

The fact was that *none* of the partners liked discussing past due accounts with their clients and they usually avoided it altogether. One by one, each partner asked me if I would handle their receivables, and it was not long before I was offered the position of collections manager for the entire firm. I had to think long and hard about accepting the job. This was certainly not a career I "dreamed" of getting into, but then life takes us on some strange courses at times. I discussed the career change with my father, who has always been somewhat of a personal guidance counselor for me. He reminded me that taking on what society might view as a "negative" position could actually be quite challenging and it would be up to me to turn it into a positive position.

Little did I know that years later I would go on to write a book on collections and would be giving seminars throughout the country based on its contents. Heeding my father's advice, I decided to take on the challenge, and from my first day on the job, I viewed my new-found profession only in a positive light. I put everything I had into learning my job. I worked for a very generous firm and was given carte blanche for whatever resources I needed to help me excel. I took numerous collection seminars, but I could not find any books in the bookstores on collections, so I started ordering mail-order books.

Mail-order books were very expensive, and I found they did not provide the information I needed. One of the first books I ordered cost a little more than $100 and advertised "everything you need to know about collections." A huge binder arrived in the mail that I read cover to cover. It was filled with useless information, most of which would take an attorney to decipher. It had a variety of collection letters. However, I knew that sending out any one of those letters would re-sult in losing the client. It was at that time that I realized what a great need there was for the book you are currently reading. Why not learn from someone else's mistakes?

Like everything in life, collections is a learning process of trial and error. However, one thing that remained constant from the start was that I kept a positive attitude about my job and about the people I called. It was not long before clients I originally called to collect money from were calling and asking me to help them with their re-ceivables. They liked my technique and figured if I was able to get money out of them, I could probably get it from *their* clients, as well. One company was trying to collect a considerable amount of money owed to it by one of its customers located in France. The receivable was more than a year old, and the client asked me if I could help. I placed one phone call, and the following week, it had a check in its office for payment in full.

I continued to accept assignments from all types of companies. At first I did it as an experiment. I wanted to see if the techniques you will read in the following pages of this book would work for all types of businesses and all types of people. I was hired by large corporations whose invoices averaged in the thousands of dollars; I worked for a worldwide toy distributor whose invoices averaged no more than $100; I called people with very little money; and I called wealthy, sometimes famous, people with more than enough money. Sure enough, I found that it did not matter what size the business was or whom I was calling—I used the same techniques and had the same successful results. Not only were my clients happy, but many checks came from the debtors with thank you notes attached.

Let's face it, though. Very few people "dream" of doing collections for a living. It is not a career you find yourself daydreaming about in high school. However, once I began giving seminars, I was bound to meet someone who did. Sure enough, last year a man raised his hand excitedly in one of my seminars and exclaimed that he did, in fact, "dream" of doing collections for a living. Knowing there had to be more to this story, I confronted this person during a break to get his story (and I knew there would be one). He proceeded to tell me that his parents owned a multimillion-dollar collection agency that he was planning to take over when they retired. Of course he "dreamed" of doing collections! Who wouldn't under those circumstances!

For most of you reading this book, however, handling collections is one part of a multitude of job responsibilities you have within a company. Perhaps you are the head of a company and have enough to do without spending your time finding out why someone has not paid you. Some of you "inherited" the job of collections, even though this was never part of your original job description. It is hard enough to ask someone to pay back the quarter they borrowed from you last week, much less call people all day long to find out why they have not paid your company.

The first piece of advice I will give you is to change your thoughts on why you find it so uncomfortable to ask someone for money. The fact of the matter is that the person who borrowed the money and did not pay it back should be embarrassed, not you. You must remove the embarrassment factor off your shoulders. Shame on the person who puts you in the position of having to ask for your money back! Can you afford to think any other way?

Secondly, find the challenges in collecting money. I have always found it challenging to take the most negative situation and turn it into a positive one. Several years ago, I earned a living as a dental hygienist, and people would constantly ask me where the enjoyment was in cleaning people's teeth. To most people, this is a negative situation. I turned it into a positive situation by finding the challenge, which for me was to take the fear away from people who disliked going to the dentist. Considering that most of the people I encountered fell into this category, I was challenged on a daily basis. However, it was a rewarding experience to have people leave the dental office smiling and even looking forward to coming back.

Now you might ask what could be so challenging about collections? Like cleaning teeth, it is the challenge of taking a very negative situation (asking for money) and turning it into a positive one (getting the money!). Imagine the challenge of having debtors look forward to your calls or letters (or at least not dread it). Several chapters in this book will help you to accomplish just that.

You can start, however, with realizing why people do not pay their bills and take a moment to put yourself in the debtor's "shoes."

I believe that if most people could afford to pay their bills, they would do so. It has been my experience that the reason 95 percent of the debtors do not pay is because either they do not have the money or they do not "think" they have they money. But I believe that most people you are calling *want* to be able to pay, but they are also in the position where they have to pick and choose which bills they are going to pay. This is true whether it is a company or an individual from whom you are collecting. Owing money is an uncomfortable position for anyone to be in, and we must take more time to look at how the debtors feel when they receive that inevitable phone call or letter requesting money. Your goal is to make sure that they pick and choose your bill to pay, and that is what this book is about—how to make sure they pick and choose you!

Make it a goal to collect your money as "painlessly" as possible. Painless to the debtor, that is.

Earlier I said, "Shame on the person who puts you in the position of having to ask for your money back." However, your job is not to "shame" the debtor into paying. No one likes to be shamed into doing anything, so why would you expect this tactic to work with the debtor? Putting a person on the defensive will only result in more broken commitments, more excuses, more lies, and, in short, unpaid receivables.

Get results from operating in the "positive," not in the "negative." This is a key factor to remember in collections (and in life, as well) and will be repeated throughout this book.

On the other hand, what about the people who have no intention of paying you and never did? When do you decide that you have heard enough excuses? When do you finally stop extending credit to clients or customers? There is nothing more frustrating than working with debtors month after month, and after six months go by, you finally decide to send them to collections. If you knew you were going to end up sending them to collections, you would have done it six months earlier instead of wasting your time and energy trying to collect from them. This book will help you to determine *sooner than later* when someone has no intention of paying you, so you can get it off your desk and spend time collecting from people who do intend to pay you.

Whether you are an independent contractor or part of a huge multimillion-dollar corporation, this book was written to help businesses like yours stay in business and gain control of their receivables. The words "client" and "customer" are used interchangeably and mean one and the same. Whether you are an electrician or an accountant, the people who engage your services are your clients. I will not bore you in the pages that follow with useless forms, verbiage that only an attorney could decipher, and advice that can only be directed to businesses the size of the Department of Water and Power.

So sit back, take notes, and before you know it, the fruits of your labor will materialize into increased profits.

Chapter 2

Telephone Calls

The telephone is the most valuable tool you can use in collections, so be sure to pay your phone bill on time! This is the tool that will enable you to get to the root of the problem and help you find out why you have not been paid. Through your telephone conversations, you will get to know your debtors, work with them, gain their trust, and collect your money. Your presentations over the telephone will be a determining factor in how successful you will be in collections.

Before calling clients, check their files so that you have up-to-date and accurate information. As a novice collector, I had been embarrassed on more than one occasion for calling a client who did not owe any money and, furthermore, knew nothing about an invoice being issued. Little mistakes like this are a reflection of your company, and they will cause people to question other aspects of your company. If you cannot even keep your receivables straight, they begin to wonder about what else is going on in the company.

Start each call with a smile

You must have a positive attitude and a positive frame of mind before you pick up the phone. It is my belief that the energy you give out works just like electricity. You cannot see electricity, but you certainly cannot deny that it exists. Just like electricity, the brain gives off both negative and positive energy. However, negative energy is much more powerful than positive energy. Case in point: There aren't many people who have been devastated by being complimented too much! If someone's negative energy is transferred to you, you will be transferring it to the next person you call unless you recognize and get rid of it beforehand. Always remember, you can't get a positive result by starting out with a negative attitude. There are times you can start out in a very positive mood and possibly end up with a negative outcome, but you can *never* start out with a negative attitude and expect to have a positive result. It is an equation that does not work.

Before you make that first call of the day, think of something funny or wonderful that happened to you. Write down all the positive things in your life. Even on your worst days, there are *always* positives. Put yourself in a good mood. Your positive energy will more than likely transfer over to the person you are calling. If you just had a fight with your significant other before you left the house, put it out of your mind before you make any calls. If sales are down and your boss just called you in and "let you have it," do not take it out on the debtor.

If you cannot stop yourself from feeling rotten—it's just "one of those days"—then find some paperwork to do for the day, but do not make any calls. Your negative mood will be transferred to the debtor, and I guarantee that you will not want to do that. It cannot be stressed enough how important it is that you are in a *positive* frame of mind before you make your collection calls. You are not out to ruin someone's day. Turn the negative experience into a positive one.

Consider the time of day you call

A great deal of psychology is used in collections, and you should try to catch debtors when they are in the best mood possible so that they will work with you. Begin calling clients after 9:30 a.m. (if they start at 9 a.m.) or after 8:30 a.m. (if they begin work at 8 a.m.). It is a good idea to give your debtors a half hour to settle into their work routine, have some coffee, return their phone calls, and so on. Avoid calling debtors during lunch hours, which can be anywhere from

11:45 a.m. to 2 p.m. Even if a debtor is in, the secretary will probably tell you that he or she is out to lunch if the person is not interested in speaking with you. You have handed the debtor an excuse on a platter. If you are calling across the nation or internationally, use this block of time to call those accounts that are in a different time zone. Do not call a debtor too late into the day or you run the risk of hearing that the boss is "just out the door" and he or she will have to get back to you tomorrow.

Thursdays are great days for making collection calls because even the "toughest" clients are generally in a better mood in anticipation of the upcoming weekend. Fridays work for this reason as well. However, do not bother calling after 4 p.m. on Fridays. Again, if they are not interested in talking with you, you have provided them a built-in excuse that they left early for the weekend and cannot be reached until Monday. Tuesday mornings are also great days for making phone calls. No matter how much a person might love his or her job, there is a certain amount of relief that comes in getting Monday out of the way. By Tuesday afternoon, it starts to sink in that there are three more days to go, and some of the people you are calling might not be in as good a mood as they were earlier in the day.

The best times to call debtors

Debtors will usually volunteer information about the best times to call, and it is up to you to make a note of this in their files. If a debtor happens to be a night nurse, calling this person at 2 p.m. might be the same as calling someone who works dayshift hours at 2 in the morning! Be careful because this could constitute harassment, especially if the person told you not to call during specific hours.

If you are calling individuals at their work numbers, your first question should be, "Is it all right that I called you at work?" You must receive permission to call at the workplace if you are calling about personal accounts. If they say no, then do not call them at work ever again. The laws are getting tighter and tighter these days and, unfortunately, not in your favor. You must be very careful how you handle your phone calls. If you are trying to reach debtors at home, call after 6 p.m. or on a Saturday when you are most likely to "catch" them answering the phone.

Keep the details of your message short

If the debtor has an answering machine, leave a brief message and be careful what you say. Simply leave your name and phone number and ask him or her to return your call. It is not necessary to go into a lengthy explanation of why you are calling. Save it for when you are actually speaking with the person.

Always remember that you are calling about a sensitive subject (money) and that it is nobody's business except the person who owes it. Never speak to Mr. Smith about Mr. Jones's unpaid bills, unless Mr. Jones has authorized you to do so. A good rule of thumb to use in order to avoid crossing the line of what you legally can and cannot do is to always assume that someone other than the debtor has received your message. Did you say anything that could implicate the debtor? Can the debtor take that message to court and successfully sue you based on what you said? Ask yourself these questions anytime you leave a message. If you are calling a company, it is not necessary to tell the receptionist that he or she works for a company that does not pay its bills and is lower than life. You are defaming the company and can be successfully sued in court for that.

Do not leave more than one message a day for someone, unless the person has specifically requested that you call back at a certain time later in the day.

The Fair Debt Collection Practices Act specifically states that "a debt collector may not communicate with a consumer in connection with the collection of a debt...at any unusual place or time that would be considered to be inconvenient to the consumer. This inconvenient time is generally between 9 p.m. and 8 a.m." (Refer to Chapter 14.) To be on the safe side, ask debtors if you can call them until 9 p.m. or as early as 8 a.m. (*their* time). Getting permission will eliminate possible repercussions.

Be specific about what to say

Take a deep breath and choose your words carefully. In ordinary day-to-day conversations, there can be a big difference between what was heard, versus what was actually said. Because you are calling about a particularly sensitive subject, this difference becomes more apparent. *Your* only objective in making this phone call is to find out why this person has not paid. You really have not given a lot of thought beyond that. His or her receivable popped up on your aging, and you need to find out if there is a problem. However, the debtor might hear a completely different conversation. The person hears that you called him or her a *failure*. Yet that never even occurred to you, nor did you imply it. This is an example of one conversation, yet you have two completely different interpretations of the same phone call.

The reason debtors "hear" the word "failure" is because they did "fail" to meet their commitment to pay you, usually because they failed to make enough money or they spent too much money. Whatever the reason, there was a failure on their part and you are a reminder of that. As a result, from the time they hear your voice, they are on the defensive, and *when defenses go up, rapport goes down.*

One way to cut through a debtor's defense is to open your conversation by explaining that you are following up on a past due invoice. Begin your conversation by telling the person that you were concerned that the bill may not have been received, or perhaps there was a problem with the product/service and you were calling to find out if there were any questions. When you open your conversation this way, the debtor no longer hears "failure." What he or she is hearing is that *before* you even picked up the phone, the only thing that occurred to you is that you wondered if there was any wrongdoing on the part of your company, not that you had to call up a failure and find out why he or she has not paid.

It is a challenge to make debtors feel that they have not failed and to make them feel as though it never occurred to you that they have not paid intentionally. This approach will take debtors by surprise. You have just removed the barrier for their defense so that you can quickly get to the root of the problem, which is, *why* they have not paid. Your pleasant *nonaccusing* manner makes them want to pay. It's human nature. You have made it clear that you are not sitting in judgment of them. They feel this and most will offer to send you a payment or at least be agreeable to setting up a payment schedule.

Give the debtor your undivided attention

When the ever-popular call waiting was first introduced, I added it to my phone system at home. After two weeks, I had it removed because I felt it was rude to put the person with whom I was speaking on hold while I conducted another conversation with someone else, and I became just as irritated when someone did the same to me.

Because of this, I recommend using a two-trunk line speakerphone that does not ring out loud or into the first line. You cannot give the debtor your undivided attention if a second line is continually ringing while you are carrying on a phone conversation. And to take another call and put the debtor on hold is to imply that his or her time is not as valuable as yours. This is not a positive message to send out. On the other hand, many debtors may put *you* on hold for several minutes, hoping that you will get tired of waiting and hang up. A speakerphone will allow you to continue working while you are waiting for them to return.

Invest in a voice mail system

We cannot overlook that it is a fast-paced world we live in and people are not in the habit of waiting for anything. Automated tellers provide banking service 24 hours a day, food stores are open all night, and sophisticated phone systems have enabled us to be contacted at any given time or place. When debtors return your calls, they want to get through to you the first time they dial. Do not expect them to continue dialing until your line is open. After all, they may not be that anxious to speak with you if they know why you are calling. With voice mail, a debtor can leave a message whether you are on the phone or have just stepped away for a few minutes.

A good voice mail system offers many additional features, such as informing you what time and on what day messages came in, allowing you to forward your calls to another number, and informing callers as to when you expect to return. Voice mail will give you an indication of just how hard debtors are trying to reach you. Are they returning your calls at 3 a.m., when they know that you will not be there? You can also suspect that debtors may be lying if they say that they returned your call, but the line was busy (voice mail will still take messages if you are on the phone). The debtors who lie or avoid your calls are *red flag warnings* that you need to be especially aggressive with them in your collection efforts.

Speak to the appropriate person

If Mr. Smith approves the bills, speak to Mr. Smith. If the controller approves the bills, speak to the controller. It is not necessary to tell the receptionist that you are calling to collect money from Mr. Smith or his company. It is a matter for Mr. Smith and he probably would not appreciate everyone knowing his business. In fact, he may get so mad at the intrusion that he will delay your check even further. However, if your calls are not returned, it is acceptable to tell whoever answers the phone the nature of your call. Let the person know that you are calling regarding an accounts receivable matter and request an immediate response. Be especially courteous to secretaries of whomever you are trying to reach. In many cases, they can be instrumental in helping to see that you are paid.

Great communication gets results

Many of your clients are ongoing and you must be very careful how you handle their receivables. It is important to maintain a healthy relationship for the few times you need to call them and find out why they have not paid. Pay close attention to what you hear on the other end of the phone and attempt to mirror people's speed and volume. For instance, if you happen to get people who tend to talk very fast and are always abrupt on the phone, asking them, "How are you today?" is not going to win you any points. This is very *irritating* to them. When people are abrupt, it is usually their way of letting you know that they are very busy and want you to get to the point of why you are calling. By the same token, if you get people who talk very slow and soft and you start talking very fast and loud, this is very *intimidating* to them. That will not win you any points either.

Being irritating or intimidating are negative actions and you will not get positive results this way. So if you tend to talk very loud and very fast and you get debtors on the phone who speak very slow and soft, tone it down a bit. And if you tend to talk very slow and soft and you get people on the phone who speak very fast and loud, pick up the pace. All these things help when it comes down to the debtor picking and choosing who gets paid.

Once a debtor has given you a commitment as to when he or she expects to pay his or her balance, send a letter documenting your phone conversation (refer to Letter 2 in Chapter 4). This documentation will eliminate the excuse given at a later date that the debtor "forgot" all about your conversation.

Every once in a while you will get someone on the phone who becomes totally irate or abusive. There is a big difference, however, between irate and abusive. There are any number of reasons why the people you are calling might become irate. Perhaps they were having a bad day when you called (and proceed to tell you about it). Or perhaps they are upset because they were not happy with the product or service, and they had called to complain but no one returned their calls. Now *you* are calling to collect the bill! They become livid and rightfully so. When you get calls like this, part of your job then becomes damage control for your company. It is up to you to calm these people down and take care of their complaints immediately. Whatever the reason is that they are irate, it is always a rewarding challenge to take calls like this and turn them into positive outcomes.

Abusive debtors, however, are very different from irate debtors. These people are actually blaming *you* for their miserable day or life. They become not only irate as soon as they hear why you are calling them, but they insult you, yell at you, and/or use abusive language.

Fortunately, I have found that less than 5 percent of the debtors fall into this category. I usually *calmly* give the abusive debtors two choices: 1) They can talk to my boss, or 2) they can talk to our attorney. The reason I give them these two choices is because, as a rule, people who are "abusive" usually have no intention of paying. And as you will read when you get to the chapter on "Attorneys and Collection Agencies," the *only* debtors I send out for collection are the ones who have *no* intention of paying. These are not people I plan to continue to call week after week.

Life is too short to take abuse from anyone, and I certainly do not recommend that you take abuse from a debtor. You are not paid to be the recipient of someone else's barbs, insults, and condemnation. Do not waste your time trying to reason with a person who is out of control. There are attorneys and collection agencies you can hire to do that.

Notice that I used the word *calmly* in describing my response to clients. No matter how much debtors may infuriate you, *always* maintain a calm, professional manner when you speak with them. Emotions have no place in the world of collections. This does not mean that you, as the collector, have no emotions. I am extremely emotional and I can feel my blood boil during many of my collection calls. However, I have learned through the years that my success as a collections manager depends upon my ability to step away from myself at these times in order to deal with the problem at hand. It is difficult enough having an emotional client on the phone. Two emotional people will only clash and nothing will get accomplished. It is not necessary to raise your voice at debtors to get your point across. It has been my experience that most people do not respond well to this and tend to "tune out" when they hear a raised voice. The employer who treats employees with respect will get twice as much work accomplished than the employer who intimidates employees. As a collector, you will find that you will get more cooperation from debtors by being rational and amicable, rather than being irrational and threatening.

Emotional debtors can be quite challenging. It is a challenge to calm them down and make them see that you are not their enemy. Be a therapist. Listen to the reason(s) they cannot pay you; you may even be in a position to help them. Let them know that you are concerned about their situation and offer assurance that you know it is temporary.

If the people you are calling become irate the moment they hear your voice, it is an obvious sign that things are not going well for them. After all, they owe you money, you do not owe them money! Do not take their anger personally and do not take offense. You are not the problem, the debtors are. Allow them to "bounce" their negative energy off of you. People who cannot pay their bills are usually angry— mainly with themselves for not being able to meet their obligations. Once they release their negative energy, you will find that you are usually able to reason with them and reach some sort of resolution.

Of course, calls like this can take their toll on you and drain you of your own energies. Therefore, it is important to get up and walk around after you hang up from an emotional debtor. Take a few deep breaths and "center" yourself before you make any more calls. If you do not take a few minutes to do this, you will transfer the negative energy (that just got transferred to you) to your next caller and you will find yourself wondering why "everyone else" you have called is in such a bad mood that day.

If debtors demand that you do *not* call them, again, then *do not call them again.* Debtors have the right to insist that you do not call and can turn around and sue you for harassment if you continue to call once they have asked you to stop. Unfortunately, when debtors close all avenues of communication, you may have no choice but to turn the debts over for collection. Before you send any debt over for collection, send a final demand letter that informs the debtor of the consequences if payment is not received by a specified date (refer to Letter 5 in Chapter 4).

If you have been calling debtors repeatedly and are finally able to reach them, do not begin your conversation by putting them on the defensive. Opening statements such as, "Why didn't you return my phone calls?" or "I have been calling you for days and not one call was returned," are not going to help you in your collection efforts. The fact that you have been calling these people for days is irrelevant. You know why they have not called you back. Now that you have them on the phone, your energy should be put toward resolving the debtors' receivables in the most expedient and amiable manner possible.

Keep a log of all your phone calls

You can do this in the form of a Client Status Report (see the example on page 28). Client Status Reports can protect you legally if you find yourself in a court of law trying to collect a debt. Documenting everything you do can only work in your favor with a judge. I remember a situation in which a client told me I would have a check "in my hands" in 14 days. When 14 days passed and I did not receive the check, I called him. He became irate and told me that he would sue me for calling him "every day" and "harassing" him. Fortunately, the Client Status Report, which documented my phone calls, could prove that not only was I *not* harassing him, I was, in fact, being quite lenient in my collection efforts.

Client Status Reports work for the good of your company and for your own good. Lack of communication in a company can be detrimental to your efforts in collecting past due accounts. Different departments need to work cohesively in order to have an effective accounts receivable system. The Client Status Report can alert salespeople or the credit department to any problems you might be having collecting from a client and keep them from extending credit until the issues are resolved. Also, if you go away on vacation, other employees can review the Client Status Reports and make follow-up collection calls for you in your absence and then simply update the report.

The Client Status Report should contain any pertinent information that may help you in your collection calls. Write down personality quirks if you are privy to them. Get as much information as you can about the person to whom you are calling. If you find out that the client is a morning person, make a note of that and call him or her only in the morning. If the client works evenings and sleeps until noon, a 9 a.m. collection call will not work in your favor. If you have noted that certain clients have volatile personalities, you can prepare yourself mentally before you place your call so that they do not catch you off guard if they run off on tangents. The more you know about the people you are calling, the easier it will be for you to place your collection calls and obtain the positive results you desire. Write down the names of everyone you come in contact with during your collection calls and be nice to them at all times. People move up in companies and the receptionist you are speaking with today might be the accounts payable person you will speak with in six months.

If you refer to the Client Status Report on page 28, you will notice that there is a column for "Miscellaneous Information About Client." On this particular report, I have noted that Jeremiah's wife had a baby on April 3rd. Obviously this piece of trivia has nothing to do with collections. However, there is nothing trivial about this information to Jeremiah. Watch what happens when you begin your collection call inquiring about Baby Jeraldine. And one year down the line, won't Jeremiah be amazed when you ask him how Baby Jeraldine's first birthday was? You may never have to place a collection call to Jeremiah again!

It is important to establish a rapport with clients, especially if they are ongoing clients who you will be calling time and time again. Show genuine interest in the people from whom you are trying to collect. When you take an interest in them beyond their debt, they will recognize the human being that you are (rather than the cold-hearted collector they may be anticipating) and will be less likely to put you off. Be a good listener and remember, the best collectors talk the least. Speak when necessary and *know when to be quiet*. Give debtors a chance to answer your questions. Do not get flustered when there is "dead air" on the other end of the receiver, and do not start rambling on in order to break the silence. Allow debtors to fill in the gaps in the conversation and encourage them to talk. Never argue with clients—this will not resolve the issue.

When you treat people with respect, the collector they will remember first when they are able to pay their bills is *you!*

Client Status Report

Client Name : *Jeremiah Jones*
Contact at Client: *Jeremiah*
Client Number: *67891*
Phone Number: *(333) 333-3333—Work*
FAX Number: *(333) 333-3330—Work*

Miscellaneous Information About Client: *Very nice client, doesn't always pay timely, but eventually pays. Call before noon. Wife had a baby girl named "Jeraldine" on April 3rd, 1999.*

Date Called	Spoke with	Conversation
3/8/00	*Jeremiah*	*Very nice—promised to send check for $500 that day.*
3/13/00	*Jeremiah*	*Forgot to send check—very apologetic; will send $ today. Check received 3/15.*
7/8/00	*Jeremiah*	*Promised to send a check for full amount due in 14 days.*
7/8/00		*Letter sent to confirm conversation; payment received 7/22.*
10/13/00	*Suzie (very nice) (Jeremiah's secretary)*	*Said a check went out on 10/12.*

Chapter 3

Excuses

I have reached the point in my career where there are few excuses unfamiliar to me. Debtors are usually quite adept at making excuses, because you can be sure that you are not the only one calling them. The better the excuse, the longer they can prolong sending a check. It is important not to let an excuse catch you by surprise and to be alert and think "ahead" of the debtor when you make your calls. Be prepared to find a solution to whatever excuse you hear.

Controllers in companies are sometimes paid hefty bonuses to stall your payment and build up the receivable. The older the receivable, the better position they are in to get your company to discount the bill. Frequently they will call after several months and offer to pay the balance in full if you will give them a 25-percent discount. Most companies will take them up on their offer because they want to get paid. The bonus they get is based on how much they were able to save the company by stalling payment. But they only stall those creditors who they think they can stall. How do they know who those creditors are? Because of how *you* handle the conversation. Debtors are paying close attention to how you handle their excuses, and how you choose to handle their excuses could be a determining factor in when or if you get paid.

There are four things you want to accomplish while you have the debtor on the phone:

1. *Eliminate the excuse you hear so that you will never hear it again.* There is nothing more boring in accounts receivable than hearing the same excuse over and over and over again. Not only do you want to address the excuse, but figure out how you can prevent the debtor from using it again.

2. *Think ahead to the next excuse you might hear from the debtor in a week or so and eliminate it while you have him or her on the phone now.* One of your goals is to speed up your collections. It can be very tedious to take a week or two to work out an excuse and find out that there is yet another excuse that will delay payment even further. Usually that second or third excuse could have been resolved during the very first phone call. Without asking the right questions, you will not be able to determine how many more excuses a debtor has on his or her agenda.

3. *Determine whether what the debtor has told you is an excuse or reality.* For instance, if he or she tells you that the computers are down and they really are down, you may have to wait a few days or even a week for your check. That *is* the reality. But if the computers are not down and this is just an "excuse," then you are waiting for nothing and you should be fairly aggressive in collecting this receivable. Again, asking the right questions will help you determine if what the debtor is telling you is an excuse or not.

4. *Create a sense of urgency about getting your bill paid.* The debtor may not take you up on your solutions, but in offering them, you are establishing a sense of urgency about getting your bill paid. Obviously, if getting paid was not important to you, you would not be coming up with different solutions on how the debtor could accomplish that. And if the bill is not important to you, do not expect it to be important to him or her.

When you start to incorporate these four things into your telephone calls, it makes the job of collections much more fun. Excuses become like a puzzle to be solved that require you to think two steps ahead of the debtor and always be on your toes. Suddenly collections become a challenging game that nobody has to lose.

The more questions you ask, the quicker you will get to the truth of the matter. When debtors lie to you about why they are not paying, they are hoping that you will accept what they are saying at face value and drop the subject. The more questions you ask, the more uncomfortable debtors become. Eventually, sending you a check becomes much more appealing than answering all your questions and having to come up with one excuse after another. The advantage *you* have is that most people in collections will accept excuses at face value and will call back at another time. When it comes time for debtors to pick and choose, it certainly becomes easier to choose you and to delay paying the people who will accept their excuses with no questions asked.

Here are some of the most common excuses you are apt to hear and how to handle them:

1. The computers are down and we are unable to print checks right now.

Given the computer age that we live in, this is one of the most common excuses heard today. If the computers are truly down, the reality is that you *will* have to wait until they are back up before you are paid. However, is it an excuse or are the computers really down? This is what you want to determine. Find out when the debtors expect the computers to be back up and be diligent in following up with them. If they ask you to wait beyond a day or two, then their computers are probably not down. Ask them how they can afford to have their computers down for such a long period of time and find out what the delay is in fixing the problem. What do their employees do when the computers go down? Explain to them that when your computers go down in your company, the employees have nothing to do. Perhaps they can give you some tips you can take to your boss on what the employees can do when the computers go down in your company. Do their employees get paid when the computers are down for so long and they have nothing to do? How do they process paychecks or are the employees' paychecks delayed as well? You are just too curious for words!

The point is, when debtors tell you that their computers are down, they should be able to tell you *exactly* when someone is coming to fix them. If they give you vague answers, you are probably looking at an excuse. The reality is that if a company is dependent on a computer to issue all its checks, it is usually dependent on the computer for most other tasks in the company. Today most companies fall into this category. These companies must get their computers up and running very quickly or they can lose a tremendous amount of money in employee productivity. Ask debtors if they can issue checks manually. How about company credit cards? It is not very likely that they will agree to manual checks or credit cards, but you are offering them as solutions *in order to create a sense of urgency* about getting your bills paid *now*.

In the meantime, if you establish that a debtor's computers are indeed down, think ahead to what excuse you might hear when you call back, and handle it while you still have the debtor on the phone. Offer to fax the person the invoice so that it will be in front of him or her when you call back in a few days (this eliminates the excuse that the debtor lost your invoice). As long as the computers are down, perhaps he or she can walk around and find out if the invoice was approved for payment (eliminates the excuse that it is still awaiting approval).

With an approach like this, how likely is it that the controller will tell you the computers are down *next* month? He or she really does not have time to answer all these questions and you have made it clear that your company has a very tight policy when it comes to accounts receivable or you would not have asked all those questions and tried to come up with other solutions. It becomes much easier to pay you and stave off paying the creditor from whom the debtor can buy some time.

2. I never received a bill for the product or service/I I lost the bill.

Oh, the wonder of the facsimile machine! The fax machine has done more to aid collections than any other device on the market. Before the fax machine became standard office equipment, this was the most common delay tactic used. Because of the age-old adage "the customer is always right," we could not argue with this particular excuse. When a customer said that he or she never received an invoice, we had an obligation to "assume" that this was true and mail a duplicate (although I find it amazing how the slow-paying clients' invoices are consistently "lost in the mail"). Using this tactic, debtors could legitimately delay their payments for at least two weeks.

Thanks to modern technology, this excuse is becoming increasingly outdated, as clients can be "faxed" copies of their outstanding invoices in the time it takes to dial the phone. After you send a fax, call to confirm that the debtor received the fax (even if you have a confirmation in your hand). Ask him or her to *read* all the pages of the fax (eliminate the next excuse that the cover page came out crystal clear, but he or she was unable to read the rest of the pages).

If a fax machine is not available, send another copy of the bill via *certified mail* or *Federal Express*. Take away the debtor's excuse that he or she never received the invoice. There are some clients who use this excuse repeatedly, and rather than hear this excuse month after month, you should consider sending all future invoices by a method in which proof of receipt is required so that you do not hear it again.

Confirm that you are sending it to the correct address. If it is indeed going to the wrong address, be sure to change your records or you will continue to hear this excuse month after month. Ask the debtor if he or she is having problems receiving other mail. Perhaps it should go to someone else's attention? Ask the person when he or she expects to pay the invoice once it is received, and at this point, diligently follow up.

3. The check is in the mail.

Find out exactly *when* the debtor sent the check, and verify that it was mailed to the correct address. How was it sent? Was it sent in a self-addressed stamped envelope, or was the check sent in a huge envelope with other information to someone else in the office? Did the debtor put someone else's attention on the envelope? (The check could be sitting in the office right next to you.) Allow approximately 10 to 14 days to pass from the time the debtor sent the check before you request that he or she stop payment and send another one. Anytime you ask someone to stop payment on a check, offer to pay the stop payment fee. Tell the person to send you a copy of his or her bank statement with the stop payment charge on it and you will reimburse him or her immediately. Do *not* have the debtor deduct the charge from what is owed to you. If he or she is using "the check is in the mail" as an *excuse*, there will be no bank charge to reimburse. If, however, the debtor is charged a fee, you have an obligation to offer to pay it. After all, you are the one requesting a stop payment so that you will get paid sooner.

Once the debtor agrees to send you another check, remember, the excuse is that there is a problem getting the check *to* you. Eliminate that problem. Consider sending a messenger to pick up the check or pick it up yourself and take the opportunity to meet the client in person. Ask if he or she would like to put it on a credit card if that is an option available to you. If the client is not local, it may be worth your while to ask him or her to Federal Express the check and charge it to your account. You will have your money the very next day and will have eliminated the excuse that the second check was "lost in the mail."

4. I don't have any money.

While it is important to be sensitive to someone's financial situation, this is too vague an excuse for you to accept at face value. It is important to realize that unless someone has actually filed for bankruptcy, the debtor *has* money under his or her control. People who truly have *no* money are out on the street. The truth of the matter is that the debtor probably has money, but he or she may not have enough money to pay all the bills. As long as the client continues to answer the telephone, the telephone bills are being paid; as long as his or her lights are on, the electric bill is being paid. Most businesses "juggle" their bills and put off whatever they can until the creditors "come a callin'." This is true from small independent businesses to large corporations. Bills are paid in order of importance.

Unfortunately, I have had conversations with many clients whose "priorities" were quite different from mine. While I have to concede that the telephone, gas, electric, and food bills take priority over most other bills, the frustration mounts with the debtors who add other "priorities," such as their cellular phone bills, restaurant and entertainment expenses, World Series tickets, and so on, over my bills (and usually everyone else's bills). These are the debtors who squawk the loudest at added interest charges, but in the meantime have no problem paying the interest expense on their credit cards. I have very little patience or compassion for these debtors and diligently follow up on their accounts until their debts are paid in full, including interest charges.

It is important to recognize the difference between the debtors who cannot pay you because they are just barely keeping food on the table and the debtors who can just barely pay their "weekly entertainment expense" bills. The latter truly are not lying to you when they say they have no money to pay your bills at the end of the month. These debtors will *never* have the money for you at the end of the month unless *you* make your bills a priority to them. Remember, what you and I may consider a priority is not necessarily what debtors consider a priority. As a collector, your job is to make your bills "important" enough to be paid on a timely basis. If you don't care when they get paid, don't expect the debtors to care.

Ask debtors specifically *why* they have no money. If it is an individual, has he or she filed for bankruptcy? If it is a company, ask if it is going out of business. This is a wonderful example of "what you heard, versus what was actually said." When people in business tell you that they have no money, aren't you really hearing that they are going out of business? After all, how can they run companies if they have *no* money? People in business do not want it to get around that they are going out of business, and this question usually gets an immediate reaction of, "Oh, no, we are still in business, we are just short of cash right now." "Just short of cash right now" is a far cry from "We have *no* money."

Ask this kind of debtor to set up a weekly/monthly payment schedule until things pick up. Explain that the debtor must agree to a payment plan in order for you to keep his or her account from going to collections. Make it sound as though you are doing the person a favor. Accept post-dated checks if they are offered. Ask if the debtor can pay by credit card or perhaps borrow the money. If the debtor insists that he or she cannot send you anything for a few months, ask the person to sign a Promissory Note (see Chapter 8). Above all, always keep in mind when you hear this excuse that if the phone is being answered, the bills are being paid. It is not yet a lost cause.

5. Hardship (lost my job, illness) and can't afford to pay you right now.

Hopefully, no one reading this book is out for blood or works for anyone who is. Things do happen to people and it is always important to hear the problems first and be sensitive to the debtors' situations. On the other hand, you do not want to sit on your receivables for an indefinite period of time until they are in a position to pay you. People in business today do allow for hardship stories and sometimes certain receivables have to be written off because of that.

However, before incurring write-offs or offering discounts, you should establish whether a hardship story is real or is just an excuse. You cannot do this without asking questions. Find out when the debtor lost his or her job or got sick. If the hardship just hit last week and your bill is three-months old, then the real question is why didn't the debtor pay the bill in the three months prior to the hardship? What is being done to get another job? How is he or she going about it? Are there any prospects ahead? Get details on how serious the situation is and find out how committed the person is to getting another job. How are the bills being paid? Has he or she filed for unemployment? Perhaps the person can borrow money from someone to pay off your bill?

If the debtor is ill, ask if he or she is still working. If the debtor is well enough to work, then there is some money to pay you.

I recall a situation where I was calling a debtor who happened to be an attorney. He sounded devastated because his job at an entertainment law firm was being "phased out." The year was 1984 and he was making $80,000 a year. To hear him talk, you would think he was a step away from living on the street. I felt terrible for him and backed off trying to collect his receivable. I even arranged some interviews for him to get another job. However, unless the interviews were with entertainment law firms (they weren't) and unless his salary was $80,000 (it wasn't), he had no interest in going out on the interviews. I was a novice collector at the time and it took me a while to catch on to this person, but when I finally did, you can bet that I did not feel bad when I threatened to sue him in court to collect our money. A check for the amount due, including interest charges, arrived two days thereafter.

There was a lesson to learn from this. If a person loses his or her job and is not doing everything possible to get another one, you can be sure that he or she has enough money to keep going for awhile. This means there is enough money to pay you and you have every right to insist that he or she does. You cannot help people who do not want to help themselves, but you can still collect from them.

6. Our computer prints all checks at the end of the month.

Naturally, it is the first of the month when you are calling. What should you do? First of all, how likely is it that a company would only print checks once a month? Well, I actually have come across quite a few companies where this is the case. It is usually a smaller company that perhaps has a bookkeeper in once a month to pay its bills and do its books. On the other hand, if you are calling a large corporation and you are told that it pays bills once a month, then more than likely you are hearing an excuse. Large corporations have their own accounts payable department and usually employ several people to sort through the invoices and pay the bills. Bills are being paid on a daily basis or these companies would not be able to function. Can you imagine hearing this excuse from Wal-Mart or Price Club? If you do hear this when you are calling a large corporation, then you are speaking with the wrong person. Go above that person and find out what the real problem is.

If this is not an excuse and the company really does pay its bills once a month, it will be up to you to work within its system if you want to get paid on time. First find out why the bills are paid only once a month. If it is because the bookkeeper comes in only once a month, be sure to get the bookkeeper's first and last names so that you can contact the person on the day he or she comes to work. Ask if your invoice has been approved for payment and confirm that the bookkeeper has been instructed to pay your bill in full. How long after the check is written does it take to get signed? Make arrangements to have it picked up or mailed to you that day. If the bookkeeper is sick on the day you call, you should not be told that you have to call back in another month. Find out when the bookkeeper is expected to return and if it is more than a few days, ask how the company can go more than a month without paying its bills. How is it able to keep the telephone company from turning off its phone? Ask if the company can pay you by credit card or cashier's check and *the company* can get reimbursed when the bookkeeper returns. Again, create a sense of urgency and make it clear that you have no intention of waiting another month to get paid.

Always call one week before the client's checks are scheduled to go out to confirm that your invoices are in its system and scheduled for payment the following week. Time your invoices accordingly. Do not send out an invoice on May 31st and expect to be paid before June 30th. Make a note of when the company pays its bills and when you can expect payment in the future. This is especially helpful for clients you bill periodically, but not necessarily every week or every month. Suppose you bill a client once every six months. When you follow up on your next invoice six months later, the excuse the company gives you is that it only pays bills on the 15th of the month (it is the 16th when you are calling). The company forgot all about the excuse it gave you six months ago that it pays all bills on the 30th and certainly did not anticipate that you were documenting this on a Client Status Report. You have caught the client in a lie and that is when you want to be especially aggressive in your collection efforts.

7. We are having serious cash flow problems.

Find out why the company has cash flow problems. Is its business cyclical? If so, does this mean that it closes part of the year and then reopens when business picks up (because that is what I am *hearing*). Businesses that are cyclical have to plan ahead and usually do some serious financial planning in order to remain open even when business slows down. After all, the company's employees are still getting weekly paychecks. Phones and electric bills are being paid throughout the year. Companies like this may not have enough to pay you in full, but they certainly have enough to make partial payments. Or are they having cash flow problems because they are waiting to collect on some of their receivables before they will pay you? Challenge these companies on exactly what monies they are waiting to receive and when. Offer to help them collect some of their receivables (speed up their receivables, speed up your receivables). Empathize with these clients. You of all people understand their predicament. If they request that you wait until their receivables pick up before they will pay you, then *insist* on good faith payments or accept post-dated checks if they are offered. Explain to these clients that you are willing to accept partial weekly/monthly payments until business picks up (and let them know that you are sure it will), but they must commit to something in order for you to keep their bills from going to collections.

If a debtor gives you an unreasonable period of time in which it expects to pay, ask if the client will sign a Promissory Note and secure it (see Chapter 8). If a company is seriously committed to paying off its bill, it is the least it can do. This is not an excuse you want to take at face value. Once you are able to work out a payment plan, you should still get a firm commitment on when the company expects to pay the *entire* balance and consistently follow up. Receivables change from day to day and you should be first in line when they change for the better.

---

8. We are expecting a big check in a month, then we can pay you in full.

"We can pay you *in full*"—that is where these debtors lure you into a trap. You look at their receivables and think how wonderful that in only one month you will never have to call these people again regarding this matter. You are so relieved that, without thinking, you agree to give them a month's reprieve because you know you will be paid (not "partially" but "*in full*") because they told you so. I confess that I have fallen for this excuse on more than one occasion, particularly as a novice collector. However, years have passed and this excuse is no more acceptable to me than the "check is in the mail" excuse. These debtors are asking you to sit tight for one month and they will deal with the problem at that time. Except that they usually do not deal with the problem "at that time." It has been my experience that these debtors rarely come up with the money in a month. All you have done is allowed them one more month to come up with another excuse as to why they cannot pay their bills. And each time you fall for this excuse, four weeks go by in which you could be collecting from these debtors.

Tell these debtors you appreciate that they want to pay you in full. However, it is not necessary to delay payment until such time. Confirm the amount due and verify that they are not disputing any part of your invoice or service. Explain that you prefer that they make partial payments on their receivables. When/if the money they are waiting for comes in, they can pay the balance off at that time. Let the debtors know that you are sure they will get their money in one month, but in the event that the expected payment does not arrive, at least they will be making progress in reducing their debt. This is the time you should let the debtors know that all work has stopped on their accounts until the receivables are brought current or, depending on your business, future orders will have to be paid for in advance.

Do not add to a receivable that you are having trouble collecting. This will only make it harder for you to collect, and the message you are conveying to the customer is that you are not really serious about collecting the debt. After all, how important can it be that you get paid when you are willing to continue to provide service and add to the receivable? Remember, if it is not important to you then do not expect it to be important to the client.

9. When I get paid, you'll get paid.

This excuse is more vague than Excuse #8 and should be treated very similar to the cash flow excuse. Find out what it is the debtor is waiting on before he or she will be able to pay you. Is it a contractor who must complete a job before being paid? If so, ask the person to send you a copy of that contract detailing when he or she is going to be paid. Explain that in order for you to extend your terms, you must have a copy of the contract in your files as verification of when you will be paid. Or is the contractor waiting for a payment on a receivable? Remind the person of your terms and point out that the contract in front of you does not mention anything about "When I get paid, you'll get paid." Once the contractor gets the money, will your bill be paid *in full*? Suppose the debtor tells you that in two weeks an expected check will enable him or her to pay off *all* the bills. You follow up in two weeks, and now you are told that the check got delayed another two weeks, but the debtor is being very vague about why. Chances are, you are looking at an excuse.

The reality is that if, in fact, the debtor were waiting for a check that was going to enable him or her to pay *all* bills in full and that check did not arrive, the person would have been on the phone with *his or her* debtor to find out where the money was. The debtor should be able to give you very *concrete* information as to why the check did not arrive. Perhaps it was being wire-transferred and it ended up in the wrong account and will take a few days to clear up. Unless you are hearing specific details as to why the debtor's check did not arrive, treat it as an excuse and insist that you have a partial payment in order to keep the account from going to collections.

10. The boss is out of town and will not be able to sign the check for two weeks.

What a wonderful way to put a creditor off for two weeks! What can you possibly say to this? Find out if the boss is away on business or on vacation. If the person has enough money for a vacation, then he or she has enough money to pay you. If the boss is traveling on business, the business must be doing well. Either way, things are going well and you should be aggressive in your collection efforts.

Is there anyone else available who is authorized to sign the check? Does the check need more than one signature? If so, find out if the other person has already signed it. Ask the person you are speaking with for the boss's phone number out of town. It is unlikely that you will get it. However, you can be sure that the boss will get the message that you called and wanted to reach him or her out of town. I have always been amazed that when people are out of town, it does not occur to them that they can actually return your call or conduct business from another state or country. It is as though once they leave town, all lines of communication are down. I am tempted to ask secretaries if their bosses took enough food to sustain them on their trips in case there are no restaurants or supermarkets at their destinations.

However, sarcasm is a negative emotion and has no place in collections. These are the times when you must hold back and "work through" this excuse. If the boss is out of town for two weeks, he or she will be coming back to an enormous workload, which will delay your payment even further unless you can get the person on the phone. This is not always easy to do. Schedule a convenient time to call the boss when he or she returns and ask the secretary to put it on the calendar. In the interim, confirm that your invoice has been approved and that a check has been prepared for signature. Otherwise, when the boss returns, you may risk hearing that the invoice was never approved so there was no check to sign. You are right back to square one.

Call the next week to confirm that the boss is still expected back the following week and confirm the time that you are scheduled to call to follow up. All these things create a sense of urgency about getting this matter resolved. The reality is that many times you *will* have to wait until the boss returns from his or her trip before you get paid, but you can be sure that you will get your check shortly thereafter.

---

11. I'm the controller and I handle the payables.

Be careful on this one. As I mentioned earlier, many controllers are paid hefty bonuses to stall creditors. On one hand, they want you to think that they are the only ones you can speak with if you are having difficulty collecting the receivable. On the other hand, they are not being specific as to why you are not being paid. First of all, if you are hearing every excuse in the world from certain controllers, then go directly to their bosses. Time is of the essence and this type of controller is clearly wasting yours. This is true of anyone who will not return your phone calls. How many messages will you leave for someone who is not returning your calls? How long will you allow the receivable to increase in size and age? If your phone calls are not being returned or you are getting the runaround as to why your bill is not being paid, go directly to the owner of the company and resolve the problem immediately.

However, if it is a large company, a good client, and you know that eventually the company will pay you, do not be too quick to step on the controller's toes. There is no question that this could make your life difficult when you are collecting on future bills. Always think ahead before you act. Going to the head of a company might get your current bill paid sooner than later, but what about in the months ahead when you are calling? How cooperative will the controller be when you are calling? How difficult will he or she make your life? Will this person now scrutinize every bill your company sends out and cost you hours of manpower revising bills and doing research? If the controller has this kind of power, then think twice before you go over his or her head. Do what you can to work with this person. Tell him or her that you are meeting with your boss later in the day to go over the receivables and your boss is going to want to know *specific* reasons why payments are being delayed and *specific* dates when they will be paid. Make it seem as though *your* job is on the line. Enlist the controller's help. When you put yourself in the underdog position, controllers usually understand and will do what they can to help.

It is not an easy job being a controller. Controllers are often at the mercy of decisions made by company CEOs, yet are usually blamed when those decisions prove to be wrong. By the same token, they are not always given their due credit when things go right. Keep this in mind and always let controllers know how much you appreciate their helping you. Do this even when the help is as minimal as it can get. Controllers can go days or weeks without a thank you from anyone; your appreciation will be remembered. When they are picking and choosing which bills they are going to pay, yours will certainly come to mind. While it may be easier to give up on difficult people in the short run, it is always better and more challenging to figure out how to work with them. In the long run, it will almost always pay off.

12. I have a dispute with the invoice.

Certainly no company is above making errors on invoices, and if the customer is right, the invoice should be corrected immediately and sent with an apology and possibly another 30 days in which to pay. However, if you have been informed of the complaint *only in response to your call*, the debtor has probably gone over the invoice with a fine-tooth comb to find anything to stall for time. If the debtor's intent was to pay timely and the complaints are legitimate, then more than likely he or she would have called upon receipt of the invoice and brought the error to your attention.

In any case, resolve whatever issues the client has with the invoice. What exactly is the person disputing? Is that the only item being disputed? If, for example, the debtor tells you that the salesperson offered a 25-percent discount and this was not reflected on the invoice, ask if he or she contacted the salesperson to discuss the discrepancy. If the debtor did not, ask why. (If someone offered you a 25-percent discount and you received a bill that did not reflect the discount, wouldn't you be on the phone immediately with the salesperson to find out why?) Do not let your debtor off the hook so fast. Ask the person to pay the invoice less 25 percent and tell him or her that you will contact the salesperson and look into the matter right away. The client should have no problem agreeing to this if the discount is really the issue.

If the debtor refuses to send you the money until he or she receives a revised invoice, then stop what you are doing and take care of the matter immediately. This is the only way you will find out if the person is giving you an excuse or not. If your invoice has several items listed on it, ask the client what part of the invoice is not in dispute and ask him or her to send you a check for the part of the invoice that is correct. Pay attention to the response. Again, if the debtor insists that the *entire* invoice be revised before he or she will pay anything, explain that you are going to correct the invoice immediately and remind the person that the invoice is still past due and that you need to make arrangements to get paid. If the client is in town, tell him or her that you will send a round-trip messenger to deliver the corrected invoice and pick up a check at the same time. If the person is out of town, arrange to have the check picked up by Federal Express. This is one excuse over which you have control and the sooner you correct the problem, the sooner you will be paid.

13. I have a dispute with the product/service.

This excuse is very similar to "dispute with the invoice," especially if you are being informed of the complaint *only in response to your call!* The reality is that if there were a problem with the product or service, the debtor surely would have contacted someone in your company about the dissatisfaction. (The logic is the same as a "dispute with the invoice." If you were unhappy with a product or service, would you wait until you received a collection call to complain about it or would you call immediately *before* you received a bill? People do not want to pay for something if they are not satisfied.) Find out what the client is disputing and *when* it was discovered that he or she was unhappy with the product or service. Ask *who* he or she spoke with to air the grievance. If the debtor cannot remember, ask for specifics. When did he or she call to complain? What was the time of day? Did the client speak to a male or female? Get as many details as you can. If the person has answers to all your questions and did, in fact, call to complain but no one responded, it is up to you to become damage control for your company and resolve the problem *to the client's satisfaction* as quickly as possible.

If the debtor did not try to contact anyone in the company to complain, ask why. Again, do not let the person off the hook too fast. You are entitled to answers to your questions if your client expects you to help. If he or she cannot answer any of these questions, more than likely you are looking at an excuse and you should be aggressive in your collection efforts at this point.

If the debtor's dispute is totally unfounded and without merit, ask if he or she would prefer to go to court and have a judge decide the case. Do not do this in a threatening way. Explain that because both of you cannot see eye to eye, it may be in the best interest of both parties to take it before a judge and let the judge have the final decision. However, never offer this as a solution until you have done some investigating of your own. Does your company have a contract with this person? Did your company live up to its part of the contract? Did it do everything it said it would do? Were any mistakes made that could have cost the customer even more money to correct?

For example, let's say your company is a carpet-cleaning service. You are sitting on a $5,000 invoice for cleaning a three-story office building. However, the cleaning people were not paying attention to what they were doing that day and nicked and scraped very expensive furniture in several offices. As a result, it cost your customer $3,000 to have the furniture repaired. The company has receipts to show the judge and it is prepared to do so if you take it to court. If this were the case, you would be better off settling the receivable with your customer than going to court.

If what your debtor is disputing is relatively minor, always ask the person to pay what he or she thinks is owed, and resolve the remaining balance as quickly as possible. Do not let it sit on the aging "until you can get to it." By the time you do get to it, you will have forgotten what the problem was and the customer will have assumed that it was written off. This is another excuse over which you have control. The longer you put off handling the problem, the harder it will be to collect.

14. We need proof of delivery (POD) before we can pay.

There are many companies that do, in fact, require POD's before they will pay their invoices. If that is a company's policy, then it will be up to you make sure it gets the POD before you make your collection call. If you are constantly hearing this excuse, then consider making changes in *your* company policy. Have your POD's made in triplicate and be sure to get signatures on the POD when the merchandise is delivered. One copy of the POD is given to the customer and the other copy will go straight to you. Attach the third copy of the POD to the invoice being sent out. Again, work within the *customer's* system. If you know what is required, then do what you can to provide it. Otherwise, this excuse will not go away.

Before you start implementing changes, though, find out if what the company is telling you is an excuse. Ask why it does not have the POD. Does it get sent to another office first? Should you be following up with someone else in another office? Should your invoices be sent to that office, as well? Ask what you can do that would speed things up so that you can get paid. Once the company has the POD, does this mean that it plans to pay you in full? If so, let the company know that you will have a copy of the POD in its office by the end of the day, and make arrangements to have a check picked up (via messenger, Federal Express, and so on). If not, find out why. Does the invoice still need to be approved? How many people have to approve it? Is there any other documentation the client needs before it will be approved? The more questions you ask now, the more excuses you can eliminate in the future and the sooner you will be paid.

15. *We can only pay from original invoices, not faxed copies.*

About 95 percent of the time you can bet this is an excuse. While there are companies that will only pay from original invoices, the bottom line is that this excuse will not hold up in a court of law. Because it is an excuse, you should work through it quickly. There is no need to challenge this company and ask why it cannot pay from a copy. All you will do is antagonize the debtor, which is a negative thing to do, and as I have mentioned repeatedly, you can't get a positive result by being negative. Besides, there are no satisfactory answers to that question that would be accepted by a judge, so why go through the exercise? Send the company another original via certified mail, Federal Express, or messenger. In addition, fax it a copy of the invoice and have the company confirm that it has no problems with it.

Explain that you still expect to get paid immediately once it has the original, and make arrangements to have the check picked up or sent to you. If you hear this excuse repeatedly from a company (and it is constantly losing the "original"), put a note in the file to send all future invoices via certified mail or Federal Express so that you have a proof of receipt. Eliminate this excuse right from the start.

16. Our accounts payable person quit.

Find out when the person quit. Is your invoice two months old and he or she just quit *yesterday*? If so, the person's quitting probably has nothing to do with why you have not been paid. When will someone be coming in to replace him or her? Is the company currently interviewing people? What will it do for payroll since no one is handling its accounts payable? If this is not an excuse, then you should be hearing specific answers to your questions. If the answers you are given are vague, go straight to the head of the company.

Unfortunately, employee turnover does tend to be quite high in accounts payable departments. This reality can be especially frustrating if you are working with a complicated receivable that requires a great deal of reconciling. It is just as frustrating for the new accounts payable person taking over. You are not the only one calling for money and his or her job can become overwhelming.

Figuring out what is due on an account can be very time consuming, and the more complicated your bills, the more time it will take and the bigger the delay in getting paid. If you want your bill paid sooner than later, find out when the new accounts payable person is coming aboard and get the correct spelling of his or her name. Put together a package of all the invoices that are due to your company. Send it to the new employee with a cover letter introducing yourself. Explain that copies of all the invoices due are enclosed for reference, along with a reconciliation of the company's account. Make the new person's job easier, and offer to assist in any way you can.

17. Our company pays net 90.

This is an excuse that is generally heard from larger companies, even though they agreed to pay within 30 days. These are usually very good clients who pay, but pay on *their* terms. Unless you are in a very specialized business that has no competition, you will have to work within their systems if you want to retain their business. Clients like these are common, and in every seminar I give, reports of this excuse inevitably come up.

Not long ago, a gentleman attended my seminar to specifically learn how to get Wal-Mart to change its payment policy. He explained that although he had 30-day terms with Wal-Mart, it usually took Wal-Mart 90 days to pay. My first question to this person was, "Has Wal-Mart ever *not* paid you?" Of course, the answer was, "No, it always pays." My next question was, "Has anyone told you why it takes so long for the company to pay?" And I knew what the answer to that question was going to be, as well.

When collecting from corporate giants such as Wal-Mart, government agencies, insurance companies, and so on, there are usually legitimate reasons why payment is delayed, sometimes for several months. Usually before an accounts payable person can prepare a check, several pieces of information are required before payment is authorized. Sometimes this information comes from different departments and it takes time before everything comes together. In Wal-Mart's case, it turned out that the company requires several pieces of information before approving payment of an invoice. Typically, it could take three months before the company has everything needed for payment to be approved.

When you are working with large companies, it is important to keep in mind that 1) they have the money to pay you, and 2) the accounts payable people have no reason to hold onto your invoice any longer than they have to. But they do have to follow the procedures that are set up within their companies and you will not be able to change that (nor should you).

There are several things you can do to expedite payment, but it will require extra work and effort on your part. The first thing to realize is that you must work within the customer's system. Call the accounts payable person or controller and find out exactly what information is needed before your check can be processed. Write down the company's payment policy from start to finish. If five people have to approve an invoice, send copies of the invoice to all five people. Why wait for it to go from department to department?

If you know that a company requires certain documentation before a bill can be approved, take extra steps to make sure the company gets it so the accounts payable person does not have to track it down. It now becomes your responsibility to speed up *the company's* payment process by getting the accounts payable person all the information at once, so he or she does not have to wait for all the other departments to send what is needed. Try to help make this person's job easier.

Many times I hear, "Why should I have to do that? I don't have the extra time to send invoices five ways or follow up on proof of deliveries. Why should I do work that *their* accounts payable people should be doing?" Again, my only response to that is that when you are working with large companies, if you want to expedite collections, you must work within their systems. They do not have to work within yours, unless of course, your product or service is so specialized that they cannot take their business elsewhere. When you are talking about a very large receivable, it is worth taking the extra time if the end result expedites payment.

For those of you who say you do not have the extra time, how much time are you spending contacting the accounts payable person week after week, month after month, finding out what he or she is missing, and you end up spending hours, sometimes days, trying to track it down anyway? In the long run, you actually end up spending more time than if you worked within your client's system right from the start.

Remember that you are one of thousands of vendors these people are paying. What makes payment of your invoices different than everyone else's? In most cases, the answer is "you"! Take the time to work within companies' systems and you will be amazed at the results.

18. We're still waiting for approval.

The smaller the company, the more likely this is an excuse that can quickly be resolved. Find out who needs to approve the bills and why it has not been done yet. Is the person on vacation? If so, find out when he or she left. If the person just left yesterday and your invoice is two months old, find out why it was not approved before he or she left. What is causing the delay? Is there a problem with the invoice? Does your client require more information? Is there anyone else who can approve the invoice for payment? Does more than one person have to approve the bill? If so, have they approved it yet? Is the invoice on the right person's desk? Will the invoice be approved the day the person returns from vacation? Is the check going to be prepared the day it is approved? Does more than one person need to sign the check? Will they be back in town at that time? If you do not ask these questions when you hear this excuse, you risk getting the runaround each time you call to follow up.

The larger the company, the more likely this is not an excuse, but a very real problem. You will have to work through it similar to the way you worked through Excuse #17, "Our company pays net 90." In large corporations, sometimes an invoice has to go through several departments before it is approved. Government agencies and insurance companies are notorious for this. Also, if you are waiting for several departments to approve an invoice, you usually will be waiting for a few people from different departments to *sign* the check, as well.

Find out exactly who needs to approve the bills and make notes of this in your file. Get first and last names of everyone you speak to regarding the approval. People are more likely to pay attention to you if they know you have their first and last names. If five people need to approve a bill and one of them is out of town, find out if the other four people have already approved it. If not, you can speed things up by getting a copy to them in the meantime. If you are planning on issuing more invoices to this company, send copies to all five people right from the start. Why wait for it to get passed along from person to person? Is there anyone else available who has the authority to approve the invoice? Does he or she have all the information needed in order to approve it? Again, work within *the company's* system. Get specifics on when the approval can be expected.

Once the invoices are approved, are the checks issued immediately thereafter? If so, make arrangements to have your check picked up. Exactly how many people have to sign the check before it can be released? What are the names of these people (again, get first and last names). If they are not available, how many other people have the authority to sign the check? The more you know, the easier your subsequent follow-up calls will be. If approval is coming from another office in another state, do not keep calling to find out if the office in your state received the approval yet. Instead, follow up with the office located in the other state. Move things along. The more you put yourself at the mercy of others, the longer it will take for you to get paid.

19. My spouse pays the bills.

Some excuses require more patience than others, but this is not one of them. You are not a Ping-Pong ball and should not be expected to go back and forth between two people. Be aggressive when you are given this excuse. Ask for the telephone number of the person's spouse and find out what would be a convenient time to call. If you are not able to reach the spouse after a few tries, call the original person back and explain that they are both responsible for payment of the bill. If your company takes credit cards, ask if he or she would prefer to put it on a credit card and make it easier for everyone. Give the client a deadline to pay you or explain that you may have to send the debt to collections if you are unable to resolve this; but do not let this receivable linger. This is not an excuse that will buy the debtor time, nor will it hold up in court. Do not hesitate to remind the debtor of this.

20. I don't owe anything.

People in the medical profession hear this excuse all the time and that is because the majority of their receivables involve insurance. Receivables that involve insurance are usually very complicated and time consuming to collect. In most instances, you must first collect from an insurance company. It can take several months for the insurance company to decide what is and is not covered. It then becomes the responsibility of the patient to pay what is not covered.

Most patients do not understand how insurance works. If an insurance carrier requires a minimum co-pay, the patient pays the co-pay, submits a claim, and thinks everything is taken care of. That is why the patient is usually so astounded to get a collection call months later requesting payment. If you find that you are hearing this excuse often, start by changing things *internally*. The moment a patient comes into the office, have the receptionist explain that it may take several months before you know how much will be covered on insurance. Let the patient know that he or she will be receiving a bill for whatever is not covered. Have the nurse repeat this in the exam room. Repeat it again when the patient leaves the office. Have the person sign a piece of paper acknowledging this understanding, and give the patient a copy of it. Take steps to remove misunderstandings ahead of time so that you will not be continually faced with this excuse.

On the other hand, if your business does not involve insurance issues, you can move through this excuse very quickly. The client either owes the money or does not. Ask the person why he or she thinks it is not owed. Did someone offer the services for free? Does the debtor think it was already paid? If that is the case, ask the person to send you a copy of the cancelled check. If he or she claims not to know anything about the bill, explain what services were performed and when, and send a copy of the invoice and the agreement immediately. Discuss how and when the client plans to pay while you are on the phone. If the person still insists that he or she does not owe you anything, consider turning it over for collection.

Chapter 4

Letters/Statements

It is very difficult to change the paying habits of long-standing clients. If they have been paying you net 45 to 60 for the past several years and no one has ever bothered to call them about it, it is very hard to retrain them into paying every 30 days, if those are your terms.

The biggest impact you can make is with *new* clients. You have an opportunity to convey your tight receivable policy right from the start. Because of this, I have cut down on the number of collection letters I send out. If you have 30-day terms, you should be on the phone with the debtor on day 31. If you choose to send out a reminder letter first, the message you are *really* sending is that you have 45-day terms. Why is that? Because you let the debtor know that whenever a bill is received from you, if he or she does not pay within 30 days, he or she will get a letter one week later, and a follow-up call a week after that.

By the time you actually get paid, the 30-day terms have now turned into 45- to 60-day terms. Also, I find that I usually end up calling these people anyway to follow up on the letters, so why not just call them sooner than later? Next month when they are picking and choosing which bills to pay, they will certainly consider yours a priority unless they are prepared to hear from you the day after the bill is due. The message is quite clear—you have a very tight receivable policy, or you would not have been on the phone on day 31.

However, letters can be a wonderful tool if handled properly. Everyone loves to get mail, but no one likes to get a collection letter. The important thing to remember when writing a collection letter is to keep it short, simple, nonoffensive and to the point. Stay away from superfluous vocabulary. This is not an essay contest and it is not necessary to show your intelligence to the debtor by using elaborate words and phrases. Speak in a language that anyone can understand. Read your letter out loud. It should be a conversation in writing. Stay away from lengthy paragraphs. More than likely, the person reading your letter has a limited amount of time. Form letters are likely to get thrown in the garbage before they are ever read and collection letters can fall into this category (hard as this is to believe).

If you are going to the trouble and expense of writing a collection letter, *make sure it is read.* First, however, you must make sure it is opened. If you think there is a chance that the debtor is going to throw your letter straight into the garbage can unopened, then do not type the debtor's name or use preprinted labels on the envelope. Rather, take a pen and write the person's name on a *blank* envelope. *Stay away from preprinted company envelopes.* A plain envelope with bright pink or red handwriting is certain to catch the attention of the recipient and will guarantee that he or she does not discard your letter unopened. In fact, your letter will be the first one opened, because you have peaked the person's curiosity.

Invest in multicolored stationery for your collection letters. Now that you have gotten the debtor to open your letter, you want to make sure it is read. Many debtors will discard the letter as soon as they see your company letterhead. However, if the letter is on multicolor stationery, they may think there is more to it than a request for money and will usually read it from beginning to end. Multicolor letters usually signify announcements, invitations to parties, letters from friends, and so on. They rarely signify collections—until now, that is.

What I do *not* recommend, however, is sending your letters or statements in the form of checks. Some companies like to do this because it is usually a guarantee that debtors will open their mail because the envelopes look like they contain checks made out to them. Since most debtors are short of cash, they get very excited and rip open the envelopes, only to find past due statements. The only thing you are going to accomplish by doing this is to upset your debtors. First you got them excited, happy, and relieved, thinking they were getting checks in the mail; then you got them depressed and mad when they realized they were not getting checks in the mail. They feel like you made fools out of them. None of these things are positive, and trying to get your money in a negative way will not get you your money. People do not have much of a sense of humor when it comes to money, and it is doubtful that the debtors will see your past due correspondence as a clever marketing scheme.

Take the time to proofread your letter before it is mailed. Did you put the correct amount due? Is the client's name spelled correctly? I am always amazed when someone sends me correspondence that contains numerous grammatical and/or spelling errors. It is most unprofessional and I am tempted to highlight the errors and send it back to the person who wrote the letter. A letter filled with spelling errors detracts considerably from the content. Invest in a book on punctuation and keep a dictionary handy at all times.

Always enclose a copy of the past due invoice with your letter to eliminate the "excuse" that the original invoice was misplaced and another copy is needed. Also include a self-addressed envelope for payment to eliminate the excuse that the check was sent to the wrong address. Make it as easy as possible for the debtor to get the check in the mail.

Always keep a copy of any correspondence you send a client. Attach these copies to your Client Status Report and keep an Accounts Receivable notebook of all your Client Status Reports. When a debtor returns your call, you can then pull his or her Client Status Report and bring yourself up to date on your collection efforts with this person. The Client Status Reports will especially come in handy should you end up filing a lawsuit to collect your debt. The judge will want to know that you did all you could to collect your money, and what better proof than a log of all your calls, letters, and responses (or lack thereof)?

On the following pages are a variety of collection letters for your reference. Obviously, the first letter you send to the debtor should be a gentle reminder that he or she owes money, and in many cases just sending a Past Due Statement is sufficient (see pages 61 and 62). If your first letter or statement does not elicit a response, each letter thereafter should be more demanding and serious in your request for payment. *Never* threaten to file a lawsuit unless you are prepared to follow through on the action.

Letter #6 on page 67 refers to NSF checks (checks returned by the bank due to nonsufficient funds). In most states, it is a felony to deliberately write a bad check. I have little patience for these debtors and neither should you. If a debtor makes no attempt to immediately replace a bad check, you should not hesitate to report him or her to the district attorney's office in your state, as well as turn the receivable over to an attorney or collection agency for filing of a lawsuit.

Letter #9 is a letter you can send to debtors who send you checks to pay off their principals but ignore late payment (or interest) charges that have accrued. It has been my experience that interest charges are usually ignored by debtors and seldom paid. Interest charges are added because if you find yourself in a court of law to collect your fees, you are certainly entitled to the maximum interest allowed by law. However, interest charges are primarily added as a negotiating tool. If Mr. Smith owes you $1,000 principal and $200 in interest and you offer to cut his interest in half if he pays immediately, there is a good chance that Mr. Smith will send you a check for $1,100. Or he might offer to send you $1,000 if you agree to write off the $200 entirely. My advice is to take the $1,000 and write off the $200. This is common business practice, and interest charges are not something you want to go after in court. In most cases, judges will not look favorably at what they perceive to be a waste of court time.

Avoid using words in your letters that may have negative connotations and put the debtor off. Words and phrases such as "neglectful" or "failure to pay" are considered judgment terms and we have *no* right to judge a debtor. You will notice that next to my signature, I use the title "Accounts Receivable" on my collection letters. Stay away from titles that have the word "collections" in them, such as Collections Manager, Collections Supervisor, Collections Department, and so on. Accounts Receivable is a much softer title and is certainly less intimidating.

The following letters vary in intensity. However, they all say the same thing: You owe us money, so please pay.

Letter 1

(COMPANY LETTERHEAD)

January 2, 2001

Ms. Iowa Yew
111 Collections Avenue
Collections, Colorado 11111-1111

Dear Ms. Yew:

We would like to remind you that payment is PAST DUE on your account in the amount of $100.00 (see copy of invoice enclosed).

We would appreciate it if you would send us a check for $100.00 as soon as possible in the self-addressed stamped envelope enclosed.

Thank you.

Sincerely,

Carol S. Frischer, Accounts Receivable

This is a standard "reminder" letter for an invoice that just turned past due. Send this to long-standing clients who just need a gentle reminder that payment is due. If payment of your invoices is due within 30 days, this letter should go out on the 31st day. If payment is not received within two weeks from the date of this letter, follow up that day with a phone call.

Letter 2

(COMPANY LETTERHEAD)

April 30, 2000

Past Due Corporation
222 Reminder Place
Collections, New York 22222-2222
Attention: Ms. Mari Lou, Accounts Payable

Dear Ms. Lou:

Pursuant to our telephone conversation today, it is my understanding that we will be receiving a check for $500.00 on or before May 15, 2000, with the balance of $500.00 arriving by May 31, 2000.

If this is not in accordance with your understanding, please advise at once. Otherwise, a self-addressed stamped envelope is enclosed for payment.

Thank you.

Sincerely,

Carol S. Frischer, Accounts Receivable

Always confirm payment commitments in writing. This will eliminate the excuse when you call in two weeks that the client "forgot" and will also serve as documentation that the conversation took place. Of course, it is imperative that you follow up with Ms. Lou on May 15th if you do not receive a check by then. Remind Ms. Lou that it was she who offered to pay you by May 15th and that you are following up to make sure that she sent a check.

Letter 3

(COMPANY LETTERHEAD)

May 23, 2000

Mr. Harry S. Myth
999 Follow Up Drive
Payup, California 99999-9999

Dear Mr. Myth:

Thank you for your payment last month in the amount of $500.00, which reduces your balance due to $100.00.

A self-addressed envelope is enclosed for this month's payment.

Thank you again!

Sincerely,

Carol S. Frischer, Accounts Receivable

This is a standard letter to the debtor who has agreed to a monthly payment plan. Notice that this letter is sent on the first of the month as a "gentle" reminder for the client to "calendar" another payment. Follow up with a telephone call toward the end of the month to make sure that a check goes out.

Letter 4

(COMPANY LETTERHEAD)

February 1, 2001

VIA CERTIFIED MAIL

Ms. Samantha Jonasi
222 Delinquent Drive
Uarelate, Florida 22222-2222

Dear Ms. Jonasi:

As you are aware, payment is several months past due on your account in the amount of $3,250.25. Copies of the past due invoices (dating back to October, 2000) are enclosed for your reference, as well as an updated statement to reflect interest charges through January 31, 2001.

Effective immediately, all work has been stopped on your account until payment is received, as it is firm policy not to continue work on past due accounts with balances in excess of 60 days.

I have left several messages for you to discuss this matter. However, none of my calls have been returned.

Please be advised that if payment is not received by February 15, 2001, we shall turn this matter over to (attorney/collection agency name) for immediate collection in accordance with our company policy.

A self-addressed stamped envelope is enclosed for payment.

Sincerely,

Carol S. Frischer, Accounts Receivable

This is a final demand letter to the debtor who will not respond to your previous letters or phone calls. If your business is service-oriented, you have a responsibility to let the debtor know that you will not provide future services unless payment is received.

Send this particular letter via CERTIFIED MAIL. (Certified Mail receipts serve as proof of delivery.) You may need proof in the future that you did send a final demand letter to the client and that the letter was received.

Letter 5

(COMPANY LETTERHEAD)

March 27, 2001

VIA CERTIFIED MAIL

Mr. Walter Goaway
333 Dont Botherme Drive
Beatit, Florida 33333-3333

Dear Mr. Goaway:

Pursuant to our telephone conversation this morning, you indicated that you feel we are "harassing" you with our constant calls and letters in our effort to resolve your outstanding receivable. We will, therefore, desist with all calls and letters requesting payment.

However, please be advised that if payment is not received on or before February 15, 2001, we shall turn this matter over to (attorney/collection agency name) for immediate collection in accordance with our company policy.

A self-addressed stamped envelope is enclosed for payment.

Sincerely,

Carol S. Frischer, Accounts Receivable Manager

This is a final demand letter to a customer who has instructed you not to call or write to him. He leaves you no choice but to take him to court and should not be surprised when he is served with a lawsuit.

Send this letter via CERTIFIED MAIL and be sure to keep your return receipt. You may need it to show the judge.

Letter 6

(COMPANY LETTERHEAD)

February 21, 2000

VIA CERTIFIED AND REGULAR MAIL

Mr. Benny Arnold
2468 Napoleon Drive
Bonaparte, Florida 02468-2468

Dear Mr. Arnold:

This letter is being sent concerning check #_____, dated _____, in the amount of $_____. This check was returned to us unpaid marked nonsufficient funds.

Pursuant to Section _____ of the Civil Code of the State of _____, unless you pay the aforesaid amount in cash or certified check within 30 days from the date of this notice, you shall be liable to (CREDITOR'S NAME) for the amount of the check in addition to (double/treble) the said amount of each check, but in no case less than $_____ and in no case no more than $_____.

If payment is not forthcoming as demanded above by March 1, 2000, we shall file suit against you for recovery of aforesaid sums and file a complaint with the District Attorney's office in the State of _____.

Sincerely,

Carol S. Frischer, Accounts Receivable

This is a letter to the debtor who writes you an NSF check (nonsufficient funds) and makes little effort to replace it. The penalty for writing NSF checks varies from state to state and the district attorney's office can provide you with a copy of the laws for the state in which you are doing business. Most states impose a penalty of three times the face value of an NSF check, usually not to exceed a specified amount. However, these penalties must be awarded to you through the court and you must prove intent that the client deliberately and knowingly remitted a check with nonsufficient funds.

Send this letter via certified mail.

Letter 7

(COMPANY LETTERHEAD)

July 1, 2000

Candy Dandy's Unlimited
555 Sugarland Drive
Dominos, Colorado 99999
Attention: Candy Bonbon, President

Dear Ms. Bonbon:

Pursuant to our meeting today, this letter is to confirm the terms of our settlement regarding the outstanding balance due to our company from Candy Dandy's Unlimited in the amount of $5,000.

We are prepared to accept $3,000 to settle the entire balance due on the following terms:

1. We will receive monthly installments of One Thousand Dollars ($1,000) until the balance of $3,000 is paid in full.

2. The first installment is to be received on or before 7/15/2000 and subsequent payments are to be received by the 15th of each month thereafter.

3. Failure to make a timely and proper payment shall entitle us to reinstate the original balance due in the amount of $5,000 and any accrued interest at the rate of _____ percent (_____%) per annum.

These terms are not an indication by (CREDITOR'S NAME) that the services performed were worth less than the actual billings, but are offered as a means to settle this matter in the most expedient manner possible.

If the terms outlined in this letter are in accordance with your understanding, please sign this letter where indicated and return it to our office in the self-addressed stamped envelope provided.

Sincerely,

_____
CREDITOR'S NAME

ACKNOWLEDGED AND AGREED:

_____   _____
Candy Bonbon, President   Date
CANDY DANDY'S UNLIMITED

Any time you agree to settle a balance for less than the fees billed, it is advisable to put the reason you are doing so in writing. Often the debtor will turn your generosity around and misconstrue your settlement to be an admission of guilt or wrongdoing. This letter clearly states the terms of the settlement and the reason for accepting less than the original amount due.

Letter 8

(COMPANY LETTERHEAD)

December 1, 2001

PERSONAL AND CONFIDENTIAL

Mr. Garry D. Linquent
333 Slowpay Drive
TakesForever, Nevada 33333-3333

Dear Garry:

As you are aware, payment is past due on your account in the amount of $17,250. Copies of the invoices outstanding (dating back to December of 2000) are once again enclosed for your reference.

We have tried to be sensitive to your financial situation; however, due to the delinquency and amount of this debt, I am sure you can understand that a sense of urgency is involved in reducing this receivable.

Please call us within the next two weeks to discuss a payment plan that will work for both you and our company. If we do not hear from you by December 15th, we shall consider turning this matter over to our (attorney/collection agency) in accordance with our company policy.

Thank you.

Sincerely,

Carol S. Frischer, Accounts Receivable

This letter is for a debtor you have been "carrying" for some time. He was once a great client, then his business declined. Or perhaps he was a friend and, as a favor, you agreed to extend payment terms. In any case, he has not been diligent in making payments, and now you want to make it clear that this is not acceptable. Notice I wrote, "we shall consider turning this matter over to our (attorney/collection agency)." This is less threatening and gives you the option of carrying the person a bit longer.

Letter 9

(COMPANY LETTERHEAD)

April 30, 2000

Partial Payment Corporation
444 No Interest Street
Principalonly, New Mexico 44444-4444

Attention: Anne O'Callahan, Accounts Payable

Dear Anne:

Thank you for your payment of $5,894.93, which pays off the entire principal on the Partial Payment Corporation's account!

Please note that because payment was not received within 30 days of our invoices, interest charges have accrued during a three-year period in the amount of $2,495.00, to which we feel we are entitled. As you know, the cost of doing business is quite high, and I am sure you understand why it is necessary for us to assess an interest charge on late payments.

We would, therefore, appreciate it if you will send us the remaining balance of $2,495.00 in the self-addressed stamped envelope provided. If you have any questions or wish to discuss this matter, please call me at your earliest convenience.

Thank you.

Sincerely,

Carol S. Frischer, Accounts Receivable

This is a letter I use on occasion to collect interest charges remaining on an account after all principal has been paid. As I wrote earlier, interest is added as a negotiating tool. Realistically, the most you can hope for with this letter is that the client will call and ask if you will accept less than the full amount of interest charged. I consider this letter "one last attempt" to collect the interest, before I write it off entirely.

Statement 1

(COMPANY LETTERHEAD)

STATEMENT

March 1, 2001

PERSONAL AND CONFIDENTIAL

Mr. John Son
Post Office Box 999
Los Angeles, California 99999

Balance due from prior invoice #99999 (dated 12/31/2000, see copy attached)	$ 1,000.00
Interest Charges (January)	4.15
Less: Payment Received 2/29/2001	500.00)*
REMAINING BALANCE DUE	**$ 504.15**

* Thank You!!!

Many times you can forego a letter and just send a statement, especially to ongoing clients who are billed regularly and usually pay on a timely basis. This particular statement thanks the client for sending a payment and reminds him that there is a remaining balance due. Use a pink or yellow highlighter and highlight the words "Thank you" on your statement, so that upon opening the envelope, these are the first words the debtor sees.

Statement 2

(COMPANY LETTERHEAD)

STATEMENT

April 1, 2000

PERSONAL AND CONFIDENTIAL

Ms. Judy D. Aughter
2401 West Fifth Avenue
Gary, Indiana 11111

Balance PAST due from prior invoice #99999
  (dated 1/31/2000, see copy attached) $1,000.00

**NOTE: IF YOU HAVE ALREADY SENT YOUR PAYMENT,
PLEASE DISREGARD THIS NOTICE.**

THANK YOU!

This is a "gentle" reminder statement to the client who pays regularly, but on occasion gets a little behind. You simply want to bring it to her attention that her receivable is past due, and give her the benefit of the doubt that she may have already sent the check and, if so, she should disregard the notice.

Chapter 5

Getting Organized

It is a fact that organization is critical to the well-being of your company and to the well-being of *you*! The more organized you are, the more efficient you become. While this is not a book about time management, I feel compelled to address this issue because time management—getting organized—is usually a big problem for people working in accounts receivable. Most people in accounts receivable are on total overload and are juggling many different tasks in addition to collections. If you are the owner of a company, chances are you are more focused on getting new business than you are in collecting past due receivables. For this reason alone, it is a good idea to have someone else in your company handle the collections.

If you do assign this as an additional task to someone already in your employ, offer some type of incentive so that he or she wants to take on this responsibility. If you see a noticeable change in the amount of money coming in that can be attributed to how well the person is doing, put a little extra money into his or her paycheck. Take the person to lunch once in a while. If you are too busy, then at the very least, periodically tell this employee how grateful you are for the job being done. It really does not take much to keep employees happy, yet I am always amazed at how many employers do not realize the importance of this. When employees feel appreciated, they are much happier and productivity is higher. The result of higher productivity is higher earnings for the company. So as the employer, *you* get more for your money. Everyone needs recognition and it is hard to do a job well without it.

Doing collections takes a lot of energy and one must be very focused and pay attention to details. If you are not organized, this can be especially difficult. The problem with getting organized is that it takes time, and time is something we all have much too little of these days. However, the time you save in the long run will be worth the time you spend getting organized in the short run. There are many books available on time management and it's worth your time to check them out. Only you know what your shortcomings are, but I can assure you that in this day and age, there is a book to help you through it.

Do you have trouble finishing a project because you are constantly thrown another one on top of it? Do you work in such chaos that even though *you* know where every piece of paper is in your office, no one else ever would? Do you use your floor as a credenza? What would someone think if they walked into your office? Would they say you are an organized person who really knows what they are doing? Or would they wonder how you manage from day to day with all the paper and files scattered about?

What does your office say about you? Many of you are probably answering, "It says that I'm overworked and understaffed." Many of you feel that since you have no assistance, what does it matter how you work? The problem is, as long as you continue to work in an unorganized fashion, you will *never* have any assistance available to you. You will continue to be overworked and you will never catch up. And believe it or not, your office is a reflection of you. You may think it says you are overworked and understaffed, while others may see you as being disorganized and out of control.

Getting organized was a problem I battled for many years. Once I started traveling and giving seminars, I was forced to quickly change my work habits. I knew if I did not change my work habits, they would only get in the way of my success. I needed assistance, but I also realized that until I got myself organized, how could I expect to give someone else direction on how they could assist me? I read books and listened to tapes on time management. One of the cassettes I bought consisted of six audiotapes. It took me about four hours to get through them, they were expensive, and by the time I heard all of them, I was not impressed. I did not feel that these tapes were of any use to me whatsoever, and I felt as though I had wasted four hours of time that I did not really have. They did not seem to address the issues I needed. On the other hand, there was *one* time-saving tip that sounded interesting. I began to incorporate this tip immediately, and you know what? I was able to save five hours of my time *every week*. That's 20 hours a month, approximately 240 hours a year!

The point is, have an open mind when you read books on time management. If you get only one tip and that tip saves you hours, your time will have been well-spent. But start somewhere. Do not get frustrated if the first book you read does not help you the way you thought it would. If it helps you even a little bit, it was worth the investment of your time. Not everyone reading this book will like or agree with everything that I have written. However, if you find even one tip that you think might be useful and that tip brings in thousands of dollars, then it was worth the time to read the entire book.

So what are some things you can do to get yourself organized? You can start by not thinking on a grand scale. This will only frustrate you and probably set you back even further. If you have ever gone on a diet, you know that starting is the hardest part. Sometimes just thinking about it becomes so overwhelming and depressing that it causes you to eat even more. That is why so many weight-watching programs (or any self-help program) strongly encourage people to take it one day at a time. Thinking about how much you have to do at work can also become overwhelming and depressing. If you think about it long enough, you might find yourself totally nonproductive for the day. Start by taking your job "one day at a time." If you are handling many different functions in your job and in your life, do not think, "Someday, I have to get organized." Instead, take just one of those functions and make it a priority to organize that one area of your life. Forget about the rest. The point is that once you get going and see how much time you end up saving, you will have the impetus to continue.

Keep in mind that you are only one person and can only do what you can do. If you are given multiple tasks to do and do not know where to begin, there is nothing wrong with asking your boss and/or supervisor to prioritize the tasks for you. That is why they have the titles of "boss" and "supervisor." Last year, four women from the same office attended one of my seminars. When we were discussing telephone calls, one of them raised her hand and told me that the four of them were taking my seminar to learn how to make 10,000 collection calls every month! I asked if any of them were able to accomplish this and, of course, they said they were not even close. I told them I did not have the foggiest idea how one person can logically make 10,000 collection calls in addition to all their other responsibilities, and they were certainly not going to learn it in my seminar. However, because their supervisor was the one who decided that making 10,000 phone calls was reasonable, I suggested they confront this person and ask her opinion on how they might accomplish this. The supervisor assigned the task, therefore, the supervisor must have reason to believe that it can be done. Because they did not have a clue, it was up to them to *"nice and calmly"* confront their supervisor and ask for her advice.

The reason I emphasize *"nice and calmly"* is because you will not get anywhere by using a whining, complaining tone about why you cannot do something. You will not be heard. You have a much better chance of a positive outcome when your approach comes from a place of respect. I explained to these four women that with the right approach, they could accomplish two things: 1) Their supervisor would be flattered that they were coming to her for advice on how to do something, and 2) their supervisor would realize that she had *no idea* how they could make 10,000 phone calls a month and would work *with* them to come up with a more realistic expectation.

If you have incredible amounts of paper on your desk that must be filed, do not think, "Someday, I have to go through this mess and put it all away." Instead, minimize the task. Think about separating all of it into three files: File Immediately, File This Month, File Whenever. Again, once you begin, it is likely that you will follow through. Getting started is the hard part. Even if you do not follow through, at least you will have ended up with three neat files on your desk—much easier to deal with than staring at a mess.

Nothing can help get you more organized than a great computer system. I do consulting for many types of companies and, unfortunately, I find that even in the largest companies, the accounts receivable departments are usually the last on the list to get customized computer programs. When I ask why that is, inevitably I hear, "We don't have the budget for it." This is always comical to me, because these same companies somehow have the budget to write off thousands, sometimes millions, of uncollected receivables every year because their accounts receivable departments do not have enough manpower to handle all the receivables when they become delinquent. On the other hand, if they had great computer programs that would allow them to get to all the receivables as soon as they become past due, the computer systems would pay for themselves in the first year.

In the meantime, there are some wonderful over-the-counter programs you can buy that can help you tremendously. I am not going to name them here for a very simple reason. By the time you read this, whatever program I might recommend will no doubt be outdated and will have been replaced with a better program. It is definitely worth your time to go to the local computer stores, discuss your needs with the salesperson, and investigate what options are available to you.

There are also several companies listed on the Internet that will design collection programs specifically to fit the needs of your company. While these programs are not inexpensive, the benefits of installing a high-tech computer program far outweigh the cost. Solix Internet Technologies, Inc. (http://www.solix.com) is certainly a pioneer when it comes to designing collection programs for medium-size companies up to Fortune 500 companies.

If you are not organized, one of the first things to slip through the cracks is your follow-up calls. If a debtor tells you that you will have your check by the first of the month, each day you let slip by *after* the first of the month is another day you have lost some credibility. Many debtors will "test" you by not sending the promised payment. Debtors need to know that you are serious. If they learn from experience that you will continue to call and follow up with regard to their receivables, they will be less inclined to delay payment. If they are led to believe that you really do not care when you receive their checks, you will be moved to the bottom of their lists of people who get paid. Each month, they are picking and choosing which bills to pay and you are sending the message that they do not need to choose you—at least not right away.

For this reason, I keep a "To Do List" in my computer, in which I calendar who I should call and when (see the example on pages 83-84). The To Do List will help you be consistent and persistent in your collections, both of which are important. If you are juggling many responsibilities or making several collection calls every day, it is not possible to remember every commitment each debtor makes. Get in the habit of updating your To Do List as soon as you hang up the phone. If a debtor said that he or she will send you a check on the 15th, make a note to call on the 14th and verify that the person is still planning to send you the check. List any pertinent information you may need to know before you call. When a debtor tells you that a check will be sent "in the next few weeks," get the person to be more specific. Ask him or her on what date you may expect payment, so that you can mark your calendar and follow up if necessary.

Notice at the top of my To Do List I wrote, "On 1/3, call Jane at Janet Enterprises...(Jane promised to send a check right after the New Year)." Now I could have made a note on my To Do List to follow up on 1/15 and wait and see if I get the check by then. If I do not get it, I wasted about two weeks of follow-up time and risk hearing another excuse. In case there is another excuse waiting in the wings, why not hear it on January 3rd and speed things up? Why not call Jane on 1/3, wish her a happy New Year, and remind her that she promised to send a check right after the New Year and confirm that this was still going to happen. Also keep in mind that for some debtors, "right after New Year" might mean May or June! Never assume that you and debtors are on the same wavelength. Always get specifics and have them clarify vague answers.

Be diligent with your follow up. If a person you wish to speak with is "out to lunch" or "at a meeting," find out when he or she will be returning and be sure to call back at that time. Write yourself a big note, calendar the time on your computer, keep an alarm clock in your office, ask your secretary (if you have one) to remind you when it's time, but *call the person back*! If the boss is out of town through July 22nd, mark your calendar to call on July 21st and confirm that he or she will be returning the next day. Try to schedule a convenient time to call back when the boss returns. Think of it as scheduling a meeting over the phone.

Above all, be persistent. If the receivable is not important to you, do not expect it to be a priority with your client.

To Do List

January, (Year)

On 1/3, call Jane at Janet Enterprises, (999) 999-9999
(Jane promised to send a check right after the New Year)

On 1/3, call Aristotle Smith, (999) 999-9998
(On 12/15, Ari promised to mail a check by 12/31)

On 1/3, send Garry D. Linquent to collection agency if no payment is received (Left messages on answering machine 12/21, 12/22, 12/23, 12/26, and 12/27)

On 1/4, call Cycleworld City, Inc., (999) 999-9997
(Past due statement sent last year on 12/20)

On 1/4, follow up with Heather, re: Tiffany's Antiques
(On 12/10, Heather was expecting some $ in about three weeks and would then be able to pay us)

On 1/4, send thank you letter to Only One, Unltd., for monthly payment received on December 29th

On 1/7, call Adonis at Olympiads Clothing, (999) 999-9996, and make sure he mailed a check (On 1/4, Adonis said a check would go out on 1/7)

On 1/8, send a monthly payment schedule to Robyn Byrd
(On 1/7, Robyn said she would agree to a monthly payment schedule)

On 1/9, call Du Yuowe, (999) 999-9994-hm, (999) 999-9993-wk
(Left message on 1/8 with Suzie Smith, Mr. Yuowe's secretary)

Collections Made Easy

On 1/16, call Smitti or Aaron Bugoff at Bugoff Films, (999) 999-9992
(On 1/3, Smitti promised to send $500 on 1/15 and $500 on 1/31—
make sure $500 went out on 1/15)

On 1/16, call Luna Tunes, (999) 999-9991
(Expecting loan to come through on 1/15 and will pay in full)

On 1/27, call Harry S. Myth, (999) 999-9990, and remind him to send
his monthly check by 1/31

Chapter 6

Engagement Letter/ Service Agreement

The engagement letter (or service agreement) is a written contract between you and your client or customer that specifies the scope of the services to be provided and the estimated costs. A signed engagement letter gives you leverage up front, and the more leverage you have up front, the less likely you will be "stiffed" in the end. A signed engagement letter can also determine whether you win or lose if you have to take your client to court to collect your fees.

It is well worth the investment to have an attorney put together an engagement letter designed for your particular business that you can then modify with each client and/or service(s) to be provided. Service-oriented businesses should insist upon a signed engagement letter *before* they begin work on accounts. Depending on the nature of your services, it may be necessary to specify what is *not* included in your services, as well.

For instance, the accountant who quotes a $500 fee for basic tax return preparation should specify that this fee does not include out-of-pocket costs, such as computer charges, nor does it include services should the client be audited by the Internal Revenue Service, require a financial statement, and so on. Another example is the person who repairs heating and air conditioning. Labor costs may be $100 per hour, but it should be made clear in writing that this does not include out-of-pocket costs, such as Freon, a new pump or filter, or even a 50-cent nail. The engagement letter should clearly state that services requested by the client beyond the scope of the engagement are not included in the estimated fee quote and will be billed additionally. Do not assume the client knows this!

Payment terms should be spelled out. If payment is due within 30 days of invoice date, interest charges will be added to invoices more than 30 days old. Work should stop completely if the client does not pay within 60 to 90 days. The maximum interest you may charge varies from state to state and you cannot charge more interest than the law allows. These terms must be specified in the engagement letter and will relieve you of your obligation to work on an account for which you are not being paid.

Whatever your terms, be sure to adhere to them. If you say work will stop in 60 days if payment is not received, *then stop work*! Almost everyone knows that if they do not pay their phone bills on time, their phone service will be turned off, and if they do not pay their gas bills in the winter, their heat will be turned off. Is it any wonder that the phone and gas bills are almost always the first to be paid? These companies make their policies quite clear. They have services you want, and they expect to be paid timely or they will stop providing the services.

For most independently owned businesses, there will always be exceptions to this. However, strive to make your exceptions few and far between. If I am a client of Mr. Jones and I find out that Mr. Jones extended credit to my friend Mary for an additional 90 days, Mr. Jones has an obligation to offer me the same terms. It is not good business practice for Mr. Jones to "selectively" extend terms to some clients and not to others. Start by making sure the terms you give are reasonable. If they are, then you should be able to apply them to everyone. Remember, the $1,000-a-year client today could be your $10,000-a-year client tomorrow.

A retainer should accompany the signed engagement letter. Product-oriented businesses almost always insist on partial payment before they place orders, and so should CPA's, attorneys, consultants, and so on. Make sure that the client or customer understands that the retainer is not payment in full for the work that is to be performed, but merely a good faith payment that will be applied to future invoices.

Beware of clients who balk at paying retainers or signing engagement letters! These clients almost always spell trouble and you will find this out as soon as you try to collect your first bill. In addition, if you end up in court trying to collect your money, an unsigned engagement letter may signify to the judge that the client did not agree to the terms of your letter and you could lose your case. The client's signature confirms that he or she understands the services to be provided and have agreed to the estimated fees. If you find that the costs exceed the estimated fees, then notify the client in writing of the additional expense. Revise and update your engagement letter as required. Do not perform additional services until the client returns a signed copy of the revised engagement letter in which he or she acknowledges and approves the additional fees.

Your engagement letter should stipulate that if there is any dispute over the work performed or the billing, the client agrees to notify you within 10 days of the invoice date so that you can take appropriate action. It is amazing how many debtors suddenly decide the work was not to their satisfaction and stop making payments on their receivables well after a year has passed. I have little patience for this type of claim and usually tell the debtor that whatever it is being disputed (with the exception of malpractice), he or she can tell it to the judge in court. The debtor will find that, more often than not, the judge will be more interested in hearing why the debtor waited so long to air the grievances than in hearing about the dispute.

Of course, if someone does claim malpractice, you should be 100 percent sure that the accusations are unfounded *before* you file a lawsuit to collect the receivable. If there is any merit to the accusation, then consider negotiating a settlement with your client or write off the receivable. A countersuit can end up costing you far more in legal fees than the receivable you are trying to collect.

Anytime you negotiate a settlement, make it clear in writing that the terms in which you settle are not an indication that the services performed were worth less than the actual billings, but that the settlement offer is intended to alleviate additional costs and time that will be incurred by both parties if litigation is pursued (see Letter 7 in Chapter 4).

Unfortunately, a substantial settlement agreement can be misconstrued as an admission of wrongdoing on the part of the creditor. The debtor begins to wonder why the creditor was willing to accept less than what was billed. Maybe there was malpractice involved, maybe the client was overcharged, or maybe he or she can get more money back by suing the creditor in court! Protect yourself (or your company) and have the debtor sign a Mutual Release Agreement, whereby he or she gives up the right to initiate a lawsuit regarding the services that were provided and you give up your right to sue on the receivable. The debtor should be amiable to signing a Mutual Release Agreement, particularly if your settlement will result in saving the person money (see Chapter 7).

All engagement letters should provide for reasonable attorney's fees and costs to the *prevailing* party in the event of a dispute between you and the client regarding fees, costs, or any other aspect of your professional relationship. Attorneys fees can reach astronomical proportions and it is in your best interest to recover these fees from the debtor should litigation occur.

More and more engagement letters are adding a clause, whereby both parties agree to go to binding arbitration in the event of a dispute. Binding arbitration is when both parties agree to present their case before a nonpartisan court-appointed judge. Both parties may have an attorney represent them at this hearing. After the judge has heard both sides, he or she rules on the case. Whatever the judge decides is binding and cannot be appealed by either party. This is a very cost-effective, time-saving way to resolve disputes and is used more and more as a means to settle.

Lack of an engagement letter or a poorly written one can often ensure a ruling against you. Not long ago, I called a plumber to fix something in my house. When he arrived, he took out a service agreement and told me that he needed my signature on it. I could tell that he was not about to start work until he had my signature. The agreement very clearly stated his hourly rates and what that included, and payment terms were spelled out. Interest would be added if payment was late, out-of-pocket expenses were to be paid in addition to his hourly rates, and so on. I told the plumber what I did for a living and how impressed I was with his service contract. I told him that I wished my clients were as meticulous as he was about their service agreements. He told me he did not always run his business this way and he was not always so careful. He had to learn the hard way.

The plumber told me that when he first started his business, he did not have very much money. He also had a trust in people that bordered on naivete. He knew enough to have a service contract but did not want to spend the money to have an attorney prepare one for him. So he decided to draft one up himself. How hard could it be? At the time, he charged $50 an hour, and his main concern was that his customers agreed to pay him his hourly rate. He prepared a very short one-page agreement that basically stated his billing rate and listed the types of repairs he was able to provide. He had them agree to pay his bill within 30 days but never listed the consequences of what would happen if they did not pay him within that time.

Sure enough, one day he met up with "Mr. X." Mr. X was one of those "bad" people—the kind who has no intention of paying you from the start. The "bad" people pay very close attention to service agreements and engagement letters and can usually recite them back to you verbatim. Mr. X had seen a copy of the plumber's service agreement and called him immediately. He wanted him to fix his kitchen sink. The plumber was at the house for two hours and sent Mr. X a bill for $1,100. $100 was for two hours of his time and $1,000 was for out-of-pocket expenses for all the parts he put underneath the sink.

The plumber received a check for $100 marked "payment in full." When he called to find out why, Mr. X told him that the agreement he signed stated that the plumber's bill was $50 an hour *period*. It never mentioned anything about out-of-pocket expenses. The plumber ended up taking Mr. X to small claims court. He showed the judge receipts totaling $1,000 for his out-of-pocket expenses. The judge was not stupid and knew that indeed it cost the plumber $1,000 to repair the sink. But the judge also had an obligation to go by the written contract and the written contract did not mention anything about reimbursement for out-of-pocket expenses. The judge tried to get Mr. X to settle and pay something more, but it was no use. Trying to reason with Mr. X proved to be of no avail. Mr. X knew the plumber *legally* had no right to the $1,000, and as far as he was concerned, he paid the plumber in full when he paid the $100.

This was a lesson learned for the plumber. The next day, he went to an attorney and paid to have a detailed service contract prepared that he uses to this day. He told me it was the best investment he ever made and he never had a problem since then collecting his money.

If you do end up going to court to collect the receivable, clear and concise verbiage used in your engagement letter can often ensure a settlement in your favor. When the nature of your services and fees are spelled out, it will be difficult for a debtor to plead otherwise when it comes to either.

Chapter 7

Mutual Release Agreement

Any time there is a substantial settlement on the receivable, it is advisable to have the debtor sign a Mutual Release Agreement, whereby both parties give up their right to sue the other party. The operative word here is *both*. For example, Ms. X owes you $10,000 and she offers to pay you $7,500 as payment in full. You agree to accept $7,500, but only if she signs a Mutual Release Agreement, whereby you agree that you will never sue her for the remaining $2,500 due and she agrees that she will never sue you for the services performed or the product received.

Mutual Release Agreements are usually used for clients you never want to see again. Your company has no intention of ever doing business with them again because these people usually (but not always) spell trouble. These are the "bad" people I wrote about in the previous chapter—the people who have no intention of paying you. As I mentioned in Chapter 1, it is my belief that the "bad" people constitute less than 5 percent of the people with whom you do business. As a result, I use Mutual Release Agreements selectively and rarely use more than three in the course of a year.

I recently settled a receivable for one of my clients in which we used a Mutual Release Agreement. This client called and told me that he was owed $15,000 from "Ms. Y" for preparation of her tax return.

When he told Ms. Y that she owed several thousand dollars in taxes (because of all the money she made in investments that year), she refused to pay him anything. Ms. Y maintained that she was overbilled and the work was not done properly. She also made it clear that she had every intention of countersuing if he did not drop the matter. I asked my client if there would be any basis to her countersuit and he assured me absolutely not. He faxed me copies of the work product and everything seemed to be in order. However, he did not want to go through a messy court battle of suits and countersuits to collect this money.

My client also informed me that Ms. Y was a wealthy young widow whose *modus operandi* was to countersue anyone who sued her and she apparently was involved with lawsuits all over town. It seemed to be a hobby for her. But there was a problem even bigger than this. My client informed me that he did not have a signed engagement letter. She was a wealthy woman and he did not anticipate that there would be a problem! Knowing this, I informed my client of two things: 1) He would have to accept less than $15,000 if he wanted to keep it out of the courtroom, and 2) a Mutual Release Agreement would have to accompany any settlement. He said that he would be thrilled to sign a Mutual Release Agreement, but felt that she would never agree to it. I told him to let me worry about that.

I knew calling Ms. Y would not be easy. She was reeling about the amount of the bill and blamed my client for the fact that she owed taxes. I had to be very careful about what strategy to use if I wanted to end up with a positive outcome. When she answered the phone, I explained who I was and told her that my client hired me to work out this problem.

Right from the start, I was sympathetic and told her that I knew this was a very touchy subject for her, but I was sure I could help both parties resolve this. I listened to her go on and on for almost an hour about how awful it was to pay taxes and why weren't the accountants able to hide her income from the IRS? I empathized with her and told her how awful she must have felt paying so much in tax (even though she paid more in tax than my yearly income). But I also assured her that my client would never do anything that would ever put her in jeopardy, and hiding taxes would certainly do that. I reminded her that, in retrospect, Leona Helmsley would have been thrilled to have my client as her accountant not too long ago. The comparison between her and Leona Helmsley actually flattered her. She began to soften.

After going back and forth a bit more, I felt comfortable asking her to make an offer that I could take to my client. I assured her that I would work very hard on her behalf to reason with him and get him to accept it. That was the perfect opening to bring up the Mutual Release Agreement. I explained what it was and told her that because she was so upset at the situation, it would probably be in *her* best interest if I prepared a Mutual Release Agreement for both parties to sign. That way she would not have to worry about a misunderstanding with respect to the remaining balance due. She could put this episode behind her and never be reminded of it again.

I told the woman I would speak with my client and insist that there would be no settlement unless he signed the agreement. She was thrilled! By the time we hung up the phone, she was not sure if I worked for my client or if I was representing her. We eventually settled for $10,000, and both parties signed the agreement. Both parties were happy, and no one went to court.

We live in a litigious society and the litigious debtor can be costly and time consuming—not to mention aggravating. The money you have given up by accepting less than your bill can be money and time saved when the settlement accompanies a Mutual Release Agreement.

The Mutual Release Agreement is a contract between two parties and verbiage is extremely important. Each state has its own rules, and what applies to one state may not necessarily apply to another. It is worth the investment to have an attorney draft a Mutual Release Agreement that will fit your particular business according to the laws of that state. Once you have a general Mutual Release Agreement that is designed to incorporate all the services you provide, you can modify it accordingly without the benefit of an attorney.

An example of a standard Mutual Release Agreement that has been drafted by an attorney is on the following page.

Agreement of Settlement and Mutual General Release

1. PARTIES: The Parties to this Agreement of Settlement and Mutual General Release ("Agreement") are (CREDITOR'S NAME) and (DEBTOR'S NAME) .

2. RECITALS: This Agreement is made with reference to the following facts:

   2.1 Certain claims, demands, and differences have existed heretofore between (CREDITOR'S NAME) on the one hand, and (DEBTOR'S NAME) on the other hand.

   2.2 It is the intention of the parties hereto to settle and dispose of, fully and completely, any and all claims, demands, and cause or causes of action heretofore or hereafter arising out of, connected with, or incidental to the dealings between the parties, prior to the effective date hereof arising out of the facts giving rise to the claims, demands, and differences.

3. CONSIDERATION AND GENERAL RELEASES: In consideration of the mutual general releases contained herein, and for other good and valuable consideration, the parties hereto promise, agree, and specifically release as follows:

   3.1 Concurrently with the execution of this Agreement, (DEBTOR'S NAME) shall deliver to (CREDITOR'S NAME) the sum of $_____ in the form of a check or money order payable to (CREDITOR'S NAME) .

   3.2 Each party hereby releases, remises, and forever discharges each other party hereto, from any and all claims, demands, and causes of action heretofore or hereafter arising out of, connected with, or incidental to the dealings between the parties, including claims of professional negligence or malpractice, prior to the effective date hereof, arising out of the facts giving rise to the claims, demands, and differences.

4. FURTHER ASSURANCES: Each of the parties to this Agreement represents, warrants, and agrees as follows:

4.1 No party nor any partnership, partner, joint venturer, officer, director, shareholder, agent, administrator, employee, insurer, lender, representative, or attorney of or for any party has made any statement or representation to any other party regarding any fact relied upon in entering into this Agreement, and each party does not rely upon any statement, representation, or promise of any other party or of any partnership, partner, joint venturer, officer, director, shareholder, agent administrator, employee, insurer, lender, representative, or attorney of or for any other party in executing this Agreement or in making the settlement provided for herein, except as expressly stated in this Agreement.

4.2 Each party to the Agreement has made such investigation of the facts pertaining to this settlement and this Agreement and of all the matters pertaining thereto as it deems necessary.

4.3 Each party or the responsible agent thereof has read this Agreement and understands the contents hereof.

4.4 In entering into this Agreement and the settlement provided for herein, each party assumes the risk of any misrepresentation, concealment, or mistake. If any party should subsequently discover that any fact relied upon by it in entering into this Agreement was untrue, that any fact was concealed from it or that its understanding of the facts or law was incorrect, such party shall not be entitled to any relief in connection therewith, including without limitation on the generality of the foregoing, any alleged right or claim to set aside or rescind this Agreement. This Agreement is intended to be and is final and binding between the parties hereto regardless of any claims of misrepresentation, promise made without the intention of performing, concealment of fact, mistake of fact or law, or of any other circumstances whatsoever. In furtherance of such intention, the releases given herein shall be and remain in effect as full and complete mutual releases of all such matters notwithstanding the discovery or existence of any additional or different claims or facts relative thereto.

4.5 Each party has not heretofore assigned, transferred, or granted, or purported to assign, transfer, or grant any of the claims, demands, and causes of action disposed of by this Agreement.

4.6 Each term of this Agreement is contractual in nature and is not merely a recital.

4.7 The parties will execute all such further and additional documents as shall be reasonable, convenient, necessary, or desirable to carry out the provisions of this Agreement.

5. SETTLEMENT: This Agreement effects the settlement of the claims which are denied and contested and nothing contained herein shall be construed as an admission by any party hereto of any liability of any kind to any other party. Each of the parties hereto denies any liability in connection with any claim and intends merely to avoid litigation and buy its peace. This Agreement and the settlement terms embodied herein are confidential and are intended to remain confidential following execution.

6. MISCELLANEOUS:

6.1 This Agreement shall be deemed to have been executed and delivered with the State of _____, and the rights and obligations of the parties hereto shall be construed and enforced in accordance with and governed by the laws of the State of _____.

6.2 This Agreement is the entire agreement between the parties with respect to the subject matter hereof and supersedes all prior and contemporaneous oral and written agreements and discussions. This Agreement may be amended only by an agreement in writing.

6.3 This Agreement is binding upon and shall inure to the benefit of the parties hereto, their respective agents, employees, representatives, administrators, attorneys, insurers, lenders, shareholders, officers, directors, divisions, affiliates, partnerships, partners, joint venturers, parent and/or subsidiary corporations, assigns, heirs, and successors in interest.

6.4 Each party has cooperated in the drafting and preparation of this Agreement. Hence, in any construction to be made of the Agreement, it shall not be construed against any party.

6.5 In the event of litigation relating to this Agreement, the prevailing party shall be entitled to recover its attorneys' fees and costs.

6.6 This Agreement may be executed in counterparts. When each party has signed and delivered at least one such counterpart, each counterpart shall be deemed an original, and, when taken together with other signed counterparts, shall constitute one Agreement which shall be binding upon and effective as to all parties. No counterpart shall be effective until all parties hereto have executed and exchanged an executed counterpart hereof.

6.7 The effective date of this Agreement is _____.

Approved as to form:

By_____ Dated:_____
    (CREDITOR'S SIGNATURE)

Approved as to form:

By_____ Dated:_____
    (DEBTOR'S SIGNATURE)

Chapter 8

Promissory Notes

A Promissory Note is a note signed by the debtor promising to pay the creditor a sum of money within a specified period of time. You can decide the length of time you want to give the person to pay the note and include the maximum interest charge legally allowed. A signed Promissory Note is an admission by the debtor in writing that he or she owes you a certain amount of money and makes it difficult for the debtor to contest your fees or dispute the services rendered should the person decide to do so in the future. The note can be secured with property or any material possession so that if he or she defaults on the note, you can still recover your money. Not all debtors will agree to "secure" the notes. However, accepting an unsecured note is better than no note at all.

There are two main advantages to using a Promissory Note. The first is to find out sooner than later if the debtor has any intention of paying you. The second is that it is much easier to sue on a Promissory Note than it is to sue for your product or service.

When would you ask a debtor to sign a Promissory Note? If a debtor wants to wait more than three months before paying you anything, ask the person to sign a Promissory Note. It may be a contractor who expects to get paid in six months and has faxed you all the documentation to verify that this is so. It could be a customer who expects to get a big tax refund and has promised to pay you as soon as he or she gets it in four months. Or it could be a patient who is waiting for a huge settlement from an insurance company in the next year. Perhaps it is a company that is having severe cash flow problems and does not see its situation turning around for several months—but does see it turning around. Whatever the reason, the debtors are asking you to wait for your money. In effect, they are asking you for loans. You, in turn, are asking them to sign legal documents acknowledging that they owe the money and agreeing to pay it back by a certain date.

Many debtors become offended as soon as you ask them to sign Promissory Notes. Their first question is usually, "You don't trust me?" Right away they try to put you on the offensive. For many years, I was uncomfortable asking people to sign Promissory Notes. My attitude changed when I realized that I had just as much right to ask them to sign the notes as they did in asking me to "carry" them for several months. There is not a bank in the world that would ever authorize a loan without a significant amount of paperwork to guarantee that it would be paid back. Why should your company be any different?

If the debtor is sincere about the intent to pay you, then he or she will agree to sign a Promissory Note.

If a debtor *refuses* to sign a Promissory Note, that is a good indication that the person has little or no intent to pay you. At this point, you might as well proceed to do whatever it takes through legal means to collect your money as soon as possible and inform the debtor of your intent.

On page 105 is an example of an unsecured Promissory Note in the amount of $5,000.00. The debtor has nine months to come up with the money to pay the debt. If he or she does not pay at the end of the nine months, you can sue the person for the value of the note. If the debtor asks you to extend the note another nine months, do not renegotiate at this point unless he or she is willing to pay down a considerable portion of the note.

Blank Promissory Notes are available in any office supply store. However, I strongly recommend that an attorney draft an initial Promissory Note tailored to your business. Like the Mutual Release Agreement, a Promissory Note is a contract between two parties. Once you have a Promissory Note that covers the legalities of the state in which you are conducting business, you can use the same note over and over again with modifications to the amount due and the terms of your agreement.

Promissory Note

$ 5,000.00

_____
City, State

_____
April 1, 2000

FOR GOOD AND VALUABLE CONSIDERATION, on or before December 31, 2000, (DEBTOR'S NAME) promises to pay to (CREDITOR'S NAME), at (ADDRESS OF CREDITOR) or at such other place as the holder hereof shall designate in writing, the principal sum of Five Thousand Dollars and No Cents ($5,000.00) with interest on the unpaid principal amount from April 1, 2000 until paid in full at the rate of _____ percent (____%) per annum. Except as otherwise herein provided, all payments shall be applied first to interest and then to principal.

Principal and interest shall be payable in lawful money of the United States.

If holder of this Note has to retain any attorney or collection agent to collect any amount due hereunder, or to otherwise enforce any provision hereof, with or without any litigation or other legal proceedings, (DEBTOR'S NAME) promises to pay holder all attorneys' fees and costs incurred in connection with such matters.

This Promissory Note shall take effect as a sealed instrument and shall be construed, governed, and enforced in accordance with the laws of the State of _____.

_____ Dated_____
DEBTOR'S NAME

Witnessed By:

_____ Dated_____
WITNESS

105

Chapter 9

Credit Application/ Client Data Sheet

When engaging a client, have him or her complete a credit application (also known as a Client Data Sheet). The credit application will help you to determine whether or not you want this person as a client/customer. The credit application includes basic information, such as current home address, home and work telephone numbers, driver's license number and expiration date, social security number, and so on, and not-so-basic information, such as credit references and names of corporate officers if it is a corporation.

The more information you have on a client, the less likely he or she will "stiff" you in the end. Debtors who decide to skip town know how much information their creditors have on them. They are certainly more likely to pay you if they know you will be able to track them down, successfully sue them, and recover their assets because of all the information they gave you. On the other hand, a debtor is less likely to pay a creditor who did not even question the fake driver's license number on his or her credit application.

You can purchase blank credit applications from any office supply store, but it is strongly recommended that you have an attorney create a credit application tailored to your business. The sample credit applications on pages 111 to 117 list questions you are entitled to request from a client/customer. Add whatever questions you deem pertinent for your business and *verify all* the information. If you are an accountant or attorney, you may (in certain circumstances) want to find out who provided services before you and why the client felt the need to change. Call the person's previous attorney or accountant to find out why he or she is no longer representing your new client (you may not be interested in representing this client after you hear the story).

Find out where the potential client banks and verify his or her account numbers with the bank. Notice if the person's "retainer" check is from the same bank account listed on the credit application. If it isn't, keep a copy of the check as a record of an additional bank account used. Ask for at least *five* credit references and have the person give you permission in writing to follow up on all the references listed. Without written authorization, the credit sources will not release any information to you.

Has the client ever filed bankruptcy? Does he or she have any pending lawsuits? How many other people are suing this person to collect money? If you are a plumber and the customer has lawsuits pending from two other plumbers for not paying their bills, are you sure you want do work for this person? The more you know about the client, the easier it will be for you to collect your money should you have a problem with a receivable.

Personal guarantees can protect you in the event a company indebted to you files for bankruptcy. More and more companies and individuals are filing for bankruptcy these days. Unfortunately, bankruptcy no longer seems to have the stigma attached to it that it once did and many people have the attitude that if things do not work out, they can simply file bankruptcy, relieve themselves of all their debts, and start anew. Little thought is given to the creditors who are left behind. It does not occur to them that their bills did not just "disappear" or get "wiped out," rather it is the creditors who end up paying them.

You can, however, take steps to protect yourself against a business that ends up filing bankruptcy. A personal guarantee can cover many pages or can be included as a separate paragraph at the bottom of your commercial credit application. Request that one or more individuals (usually the corporate officer, principal owner, or partner of the partnership) give a personal written guarantee that he or she will be personally liable in the event that the company cannot meet its obligations to you. Even though a company files bankruptcy, many owners come out of the experience virtually unscathed. More than likely they have protected themselves in the event of bankruptcy. And you too will be protected because you were smart enough to get a personal guarantee.

Pay attention to any questions the potential client did not answer. Did he or she list only three credit references when you asked for five? The more blanks, the bigger the risk if you decide to take this person on as a client. Above all, there is no point in having him or her fill out a credit application unless you plan to follow up on all the items listed. Be diligent about this. The fastest way to verify information on the credit application is to use credit-reporting organizations such as TRW, Equifax, and Dun & Bradstreet. There are also many specialized industry credit-reporting agencies listed on the Internet that are competitive in price, as well.

The comprehensive credit application filled out by the debtor could be your biggest asset if you find yourself with a judgment against him or her in the end.

The Frischer Company

Credit Application
(Commercial)

Date_____

A) Firm or Business Name_____

B) Doing Business As (DBA)_____

C) Billing Address_____City_____State_____ZIP_____

D) Shipping Address_____City_____State_____ZIP_____

E) Phone Number_____ F) Fax Number_____

G) E-Mail Address_____

   **Please list all branch and/or affiliate store addresses on back of application

H) Ownership (Name or Parent Company, if Subsidiary)_____

   ___Proprietorship   ___Partnership   ___Closely Held Corp.
   ___Widely Held Corp.   ___Subsidiary

I) Proprietor, Partners, or Officers, if incorporated
   Name_____ Home Address_____
   SSN#_____
   Name_____ Home Address_____
   SSN#_____
   Name_____ Home Address_____
   SSN#_____

J) Federal Tax or Social Security Number_____
   Principal Business of Firm_____

K) Year Business Established_____ At present location since_____

L) Is business incorporated?_____ If so, under laws of what state?_____

M) Pending Lawsuits Against Company (if so, please explain):
   _____
   _____

N) List employees names and titles who can authorize purchase orders for your company:
   1)_____
   2)_____

3)_____

4)_____

5)_____

6)_____

(Please list additional names on the back of this application)

CREDIT INFORMATION:

O) Estimated Sales for 12 months: $_____

P) Estimated Maximum Credit Desired: _____

Q) Name of Bank_____ Name of Bank_____
    Address_____ Address_____
    City, ST_____ City, ST_____
    Account Number_____ Account Number_____

CREDIT REFERENCES:

R) Name_____ 4) Name_____
   Address_____ Address_____
   City, ST_____ City, ST_____
   Phone Number_____ Phone Number_____
   For How Long_____ For How Long_____

2) Name_____ 5) Name_____
   Address_____ Address_____
   City, ST_____ City, ST_____
   Phone Number_____ Phone Number_____
   For How Long_____ For How Long_____

3) Name_____ 6) Name_____
   Address_____ Address_____
   City, ST_____ City, ST_____
   Phone Number_____ Phone Number_____
   For How Long_____ For How Long_____

S) I HEREBY WARRANT THAT THE ABOVE INFORMATION IS TRUE AND CORRECT, AND IS FURNISHED FOR THE PURPOSE OF OBTAINING CREDIT. I HEREBY AGREE THAT **THE FRISCHER COMPANY** MAY INVESTIGATE OUR CREDIT RECORD AND THAT, IF AN ACCOUNT IS OPENED, **THE FRISCHER COMPANY** MAY FURNISH INFORMATION REGARDING THIS ACCOUNT TO CREDIT REPORTING AGENCIES AND OTHERS WHO MAY PROPERLY REQUEST SUCH INFORMATION. MY SIGNATURE BELOW AUTHORIZES ANY AND ALL AGENCIES LISTED ON THIS APPLICATION AS A CREDIT REFERENCE TO RELEASE INFORMATION ABOUT OUR COMPANY'S CREDIT HISTORY WITH THEM.

COMPANY NAME_____

NAME_____ DATE_____

TITLE_____

The Frischer Company

Credit Application
(Individual)

Date_____

Name_____
Last   First   Middle

Home Address (do not use a post office box):

_____
Street   City   State   ZIP Code

Mailing Address:

_____
Street   City   State   ZIP Code

At current addresss since_____

Do you own or rent your home? _____Own   _____Rent

Former Address (if less than two years):

_____

Home Phone Number_____ Work Phone Number_____
Fax Number(s): Home_____ Work_____
E-mail Address(es) _____

_____

Social Security Number_____ Birth Date_____

Driver's License_____ Expiration Date_____
(Number)   (State)

Mother's Maiden Name_____

Have you ever declared bankruptcy? Yes_____ No_____
If yes, what year? _____

Has the bankruptcy been discharged? Yes_____ No_____

Pending Lawsuits (if yes, please explain):

_____
_____

EMPLOYMENT INFORMATION

Employer_____ Phone #_____
Address_____

Position_____

How Long Employed_____ Monthly Salary_____

Previous Employer (if employed less than 3 years)
_____ Phone #_____
Address_____

Source of Other Income (please explain):

_____
_____
_____
_____

SPOUSAL INFORMATION

Spouse's Name_____
                    Last   First   Middle

Spouse's Social Security Number_____

Spouse's Work Phone_____

BANK REFERENCES

Name of Bank_____ Name of Bank_____
Address_____ Address_____
City, ST_____ City, ST_____
Account Number: Account Number:
    Checking_____   Checking_____
    Savings_____   Savings_____

CREDIT REFERENCES

AMERICAN EXPRESS
    Account Number(s)_____

VISA
    Account Number(s)_____

MASTERCARD
    Account Number(s)_____

DEPARTMENT STORES
    Name_____ Account Number_____
    Name_____ Account Number_____
    Name_____ Account Number_____
    Name_____ Account Number_____

OTHER
    Name_____ Account Number_____
    Name_____ Account Number_____
    Name_____ Account Number_____

I HEREBY WARRANT THAT THE ABOVE INFORMATION IS TRUE AND CORRECT, AND IS FURNISHED FOR THE PURPOSE OF OBTAINING CREDIT. I HEREBY AGREE THAT **THE FRISCHER COMPANY** MAY INVESTIGATE MY CREDIT RECORD AND THAT, IF AN ACCOUNT IS OPENED, **THE FRISCHER COMPANY** MAY FURNISH INFORMATION

REGARDING THIS ACCOUNT TO CREDIT REPORTING AGENCIES
AND OTHERS WHO MAY PROPERLY REQUEST SUCH INFORMATION.
MY SIGNATURE BELOW AUTHORIZES ANY AND ALL AGENCIES
LISTED ON THIS APPLICATION AS A CREDIT REFERENCE TO
RELEASE INFORMATION ABOUT MY CREDIT HISTORY WITH THEM.

NAME_____ DATE_____

Personal Guarantee

FOR GOOD CONSIDERATION, the undersigned does hereby guarantee to (Creditor) the prompt, punctual, and full payment of all present and future indebtedness to (Creditor) from (Customer) according to the tenor of the within agreement and, in the event of default, authorizes any holder hereof to proceed against the undersigned, for the full amount due including reasonable attorneys' fees and costs necessary for collection and enforcement of this guaranty, and hereby waives presentment, demand, protest, notice of protest, notice of dishonor, and any and all other notices or demand of whatever character to which the undersigned might otherwise be entitled. The undersigned further consents to any extension granted by any holder and waives notice thereof.

The obligations of the undersigned shall at the election of (Creditor) be primary and not necessarily secondary and (Creditor) shall not be required to exhaust its remedies as against (Customer) prior to enforcing its rights under this guaranty against the undersigned.

The guaranty hereunder shall be unconditional and absolute and the undersigned waive all rights of subrogation and set-off until all sums due under this guaranty are fully paid. The undersigned agrees to remain fully bound until fully paid, and waives all suretyship defenses or defenses in the nature thereof, generally.

This guaranty may be terminated by any guarantor upon fifteen (15) days written notice of termination, mailed certified mail, return receipt requested to the Creditor. Such termination shall extend only to credit extended beyond said fifteen (15) day period and not to prior extended credit.

If more than one guarantor, obligation of each shall be joint and several and binding upon and inure to the benefit of the parties, their successors, assigns, and personal representatives. Each of the undersigned warrants and represents it has full authority to enter into this guaranty. Termination of this guaranty by any guarantor shall not impair the continuing guaranty of any remaining guarantors of said termination.

This guaranty shall be construed and enforced under the laws of the State of _____.

WITNESS the hand and seal of the undersigned this _____ (Day) of _____ (Year).

Witness.......................... Name of Guarantor ....

Residence..

....

Business Address..

....

Customer Name..

Chapter 10

Invoices

While this book is primarily concerned with how to collect past due invoices, it is important to take a look at the invoices themselves. There are two things that should be *prominently displayed* on an invoice: the *amount* due and *when* it is due. Even though the client has agreed to your terms by signing your engagement letter or service agreement, terms should appear on every invoice.

The days of conspicuous consumption are over, and I find that invoices are scrutinized more than ever. Clients and customers ask more questions, want more detail, and in general, want to know what they are getting for their money.

If a client requests a detailed bill, including a breakdown of the hours worked on his or her account, and receives an invoice for "general services rendered," do not be surprised if the person withholds payment until you revise the invoice to his or her satisfaction. Make a notation to whoever prepares the bill that this particular client requests a breakdown of hours worked on his or her account to be attached to the invoice.

Proofread all invoices before they are mailed. Are the descriptions accurate? Do the numbers add up correctly? Get it right *before* you send out the invoice or you will be spending needless time making corrections. In situations like these, payment can be delayed even further because there is the question of whether the client has another 30 days in which to pay the corrected invoice.

Are your invoices sent in a timely fashion? If the client receives your invoice and has completely forgotten what you did, then your invoices are not being sent in a timely manner. Ideally, an invoice should be presented upon completion of the work product. Every day you wait beyond that is a delay in your receivable. A client who receives an invoice along with the work product is more likely to pay the invoice on time than the client who receives an invoice three months down the line. He or she already has the work product and you have removed the sense of urgency with regard to paying your invoice. The client has other more "pressing" bills to pay and your invoice can just wait until something else is needed from you. After all, the person does not even remember what it was you did in the first place.

A few years ago, I was trying to collect a past due receivable from a company that distributed stationery and office supplies. In fact, the company I worked for bought all its paper products from this client, so we were its customer, as well. This was an ongoing client and we billed it monthly. It seemed like I was always trying to collect its receivable and was constantly told of severe cash flow problems.

Out of curiosity, I looked in our files to see how often this company billed us for the products we purchased. I was astounded to see that we were billed about two months after the products were delivered to our office. No wonder this company had "severe" cash flow problems! I met with the president of the company and brought the matter to his attention. He was so busy "running" the company, he had absolutely no idea that the company's invoices were being sent out so late. He hired me to consult with his billing department and determine the cause of the delay in getting the invoices out. It took several months to turn the billing system around, but eventually we had the invoices going out with the delivered products. The company's cash flow picked up tremendously and, of course, I no longer had a problem collecting its receivable. When your invoices are sent out in a timely fashion, you will be amazed at the improvement in your cash flow.

Chapter 11

The Frischer Report

What about the clients who have been faithful and profitable customers for a considerable period of time but who suddenly find themselves in dire financial straits that may or may not be temporary? There was a time when the support of these people kept your company going, and many partners or owners feel a moral obligation to help them through their hard times. Regardless of company policy, it is not always easy to "cut" these clients off.

Even if the company in which you are working has a policy that work is to stop if accounts remain delinquent after 60 days, you will inevitably find clients who become "exceptions" to this policy. Perhaps these clients are long-time friends of an owner of your company, or perhaps they referred a great amount of business to the company in years past. In any case, the collections manager may be instructed not to call these clients or get involved in collecting the receivables.

The problem is that the situation can get out of control, particularly in a large company. If there are 10 partners and each partner is "carrying" the receivable of two or three clients, you could have a significant accounts receivable problem. Many times a partner intends to "carry" a client for just a few months until things turn around. However, time marches on, and before you know it, a "few months" have turned into a year and the receivable is now twice what it was 12 months ago.

If you are a collections manager, you have an obligation to let the partners know when a receivable is getting out of hand and inform them of just how long it has been delinquent. When one partner's receivable is delinquent, it has an impact on all of them and they should be in agreement on whether or not to carry a client.

Keeping this in mind, I created The Frischer Report. This report was originally geared toward larger companies where more than one partner had a vested interest in the welfare of the company. However, I now issue the report even when there is only one person in charge. The report can be issued annually, semi-annually, or even monthly. It is a comprehensive look at clients who have balances long overdue, yet their work is still ongoing.

The report lists active clients who are delinquent in their accounts receivable by 90 days or more. Partners have a chance to review other partners' "problem clients," and collectively they can decide if work should continue or if work should stop until payment is received. Through this report, you can offer your opinion on problem clients, based upon how difficult it has been to collect their receivables. Partners can get so busy that they do not have time to get a "big" picture of what is going on in their company. The Frischer Report puts the big picture at their fingertips.

Your job becomes even more frustrating when you continue to chip away at the aging, yet every month when your new aging comes out, the numbers have increased! This is when many accounts receivable people are confronted by their bosses, who want to know how they can be doing their jobs efficiently when the aging keeps going up.

The Frischer Report is especially effective if you work for a company where salespeople are able to arbitrarily add to delinquent accounts. To protect my job and myself, I started preparing a monthly Frischer Report for the partners that showed the *cumulative* effect of all the accounts everyone was telling me not to worry about. Reasons were then given why (in my opinion) I felt that they should stop work on these particular accounts. Collectively the partners could then decide what they wanted to do. Because they owned the company, this was their decision to make, not mine.

My opinions were taken more seriously once the cumulative effect was brought to the partners' attention. They were no longer looking at a $5,000 or $10,000 receivable; now they were looking at a $100,000 receivable that was getting larger every day!

Once you begin incorporating the Frischer Report as part of your job responsibility, you will be able to give your boss an accurate reading of your job performance. Each time a new aging comes out, take the total and deduct the receivables of customers listed on your Frischer Report. For example, last month, you noticed that a particular receivable in the amount of $5,000 became 90 days past due. You were having problems collecting on this account and immediately issued a report recommending that work stop (including the reasons why). If a month goes by and this same receivable has now increased to $10,000 on your new aging report, deduct $5,000 from your aging.

After all, if the powers that be had listened to you, your aging would not have increased by $5,000. As long as you protected your position by documenting it in a report (or in a memo), there is no reason you should be penalized for the increase in these receivables. By the time you finish deducting these increases, you will find that an accurate reading of your aging will more than likely show that the numbers have actually gone down from the previous month.

The Frischer Report will not only back you up in writing and ensure that you are judged solely on your performance, but it also works for the good of your company. You have an obligation to your employer(s) to bring to their attention customers who appear to be out of control. Do not "assume" that they are on top of this. As busy as *you* are, the people in charge are usually that much busier running the company. Part of your expertise in collections is being able to spot problem accounts and determine when a customer has no intention of paying you. A portion of your salary is based upon that expertise; consider yourself the watchdog for your company's collections. It is not your concern whether your advice is taken. Continue to do your job and bring problem accounts to the attention of whoever is in charge.

The following is a fictitious example of The Frischer Report. Any similarity to real people is purely coincidental.

The Frischer Report

Cumulative Effect on Aging Report: $66,800

December, 2000

Partner Norm:

U.R. Late Productions—After a good deal of negotiating (and the threat of a lawsuit), client has agreed to pay the $8,000 he owes us over a six-month period beginning in January. We should be paid *in advance* for any work performed subsequent to that.

Partner Ruth:

Dr. S. Lowpey—Dr. Lowpey currently owes $6,000 and he has been sending us monthly payments of $500. However, at this rate, his receivable will not be down to zero for another 12 months (as long as we don't add to it). If we are to continue servicing Dr. Lowpey's account, we should be paid *in advance* for future services.

Lesis Moore—I will reiterate what I said on last year's Frischer Report: "Nice man, doesn't pay timely" (receivable is now up to $7,500).

Information Unlimited—This client came to us this year and although she paid us a $1,000 retainer, she has used it up and is slipping fast on my aging. This client is now six months past due and currently owes us $5,000. She agreed to make payments of $500 a month, which she was diligent about sending until last month, when we received nothing. We continue to bill well in excess of $500 a month. Last month we billed her $1,200 and this month we billed another $1,000. This is a potential problem and yet we continue to do work for her. What happened to our 60-day policy of stopping work on accounts over 60 days past due?

Partner Alan:

Tom Kvetchit—Partner Kathryn needs to call Tom and find out (once again) why he has a problem paying our bills. Receivable is not up to $3,500,00. I cannot recall Tom ever paying a bill without complaining about it for months before he pays. Maybe we should put Tom on a "fixed" fee arrangement and establish fees and costs before work begins so that he stops wasting everyone's time.

Melvin B. Elvin—When a client won't pay the first invoice of $105 (last June), this is an indication of a problem. Receivable is now up to $5,000. *All work should stop on this account,* if it hasn't already, in accordance with firm policy. Note: Client balked at paying a retainer and is now balking at paying his bill (not a surprise). Partners must *insist* on retainers.

Mega Films—Mega Films is a fairly new client and we are in a position to insist that it pays timely (it is three months behind and now owes $2,300). Otherwise, this could be a potential problem.

Bruce S. Nail—*Very* slow pay. Owes us $4,500 and $4,000 is over 90 days old. Partner Alan should get paid in advance for any future work (or upon receipt of the work product), along with a weekly payment plan against balance due.

Ty T. Wad—Ty ignores calls, letters, and past due statements. I realize his net worth is in excess of one million dollars. However, we are not seeing any of it. No more work should be done until he brings his account current. Receivable now exceeds $12,000.

Partner Mike:

Marlena D. Trick—Marlena is on a monthly retainer of $300, which she always pays on time. However, I have noticed that $650 is being run through the work in process each month (for the past three months) and we are taking a monthly loss of $350 on this account. If work is to continue at this pace, Marlena's retainer should be renegotiated and increased to $650 a month so we do not take a loss.

Nancy Mae—Nancy is on a retainer of $500 a month. There is currently $12,000 in work-in-process (unbilled). If we never add another penny to this account, Nancy's work-in-process will be used up in two years. A supplemental bill should be sent to Nancy in addition to her $500/month retainer. Obviously, more work was done for her than was anticipated (check engagement letter to see what services we included for $500 a month).

Gold Crown's Incorporated—Dr. Tooth has been a long-standing client and is responsible for Gold Crown's $5,000 receivable, which is *several* months past due. Dr. Tooth is trying to get a line of credit and will then pay us a "few thousand" dollars. Getting the entire balance paid will take some time, though, and any future work to be done for Gold Crown is not likely to be paid off too soon.

Partner Ina:

NSF Productions—Accounts receivable is at $5,000 and I am sure this will end up in small claims court. This client bounced a check on us twice last year. Client finally paid when I told him that bouncing a check was against the law and I would turn the matter over to the district attorney and let that office handle it. The client paid shortly thereafter. All work should stop until we are paid, and the receivable should be vigorously pursued.

Partner Vern:

Harry's Fix-It, Inc.—Harry is paying down his $3,000 receivable by sending us $500 a month. However, work in progress is going strong at $400 a month. Partner Ina should speak with Harry and have him increase his monthly payments to $1,000 so he can catch up on his receivable. Perhaps we have something for Harry to "fix" to offset his receivable (?).

Chapter 12

Collection Agencies

When should you use a collection agency? There are times when a debtor will simply not take or return your call and there comes a point when it is futile for you to keep calling. Only you can be the judge of when that is. If you have left several messages for a client and he or she has not called you back within three to four weeks (which takes into consideration that the person might have been on vacation), it is quite obvious that either you are not at the top of his or her list of priorities or the client has no intention of calling you back. Even if debtors have no news to give about when they expect to send you checks, they still owe you the courtesy of returning your calls. Your time is valuable and each day you are unable to reach a client is another day you have not been paid.

When all avenues of communication have been exhausted, this is the time you may want to think about engaging a collection agency.

Most people think of collection agencies in a negative sense. However, there are many credible collection agencies out there that, for a minimal investment on your part, can be used as a tremendous tool to assist you in collecting significant amounts of money. Take the time to contact several collection agencies and hear what each has to offer. It is best to use a reputable long-standing collection agency that you can trust. The agency should be a member of both national trade associations, Associated Credit Bureaus (ACB) and American Collectors Association (ACA).

These organizations provide all important standards and training and require the agencies to abide by the Fair Debt Collection Practices Act (see Chapter 14) and to follow the guidelines of state and federal laws. Make sure the collection agency you choose is insured, licensed, and bonded, as well as licensed to collect in other states. Find out if it has handled collections from businesses similar to yours and ask for references.

I especially recommend the letter-writing service offered from nationally known collection agencies, such as Dun & Bradstreet, I.C. System, or Transworld Systems, Inc. For a fixed fee, they will send out a series of letters (usually five) requesting payment. Their final demand letter may be from a licensed practicing attorney. Some collection agencies charge as little as $15 per account for this service. Beyond that, whatever you are able to collect from a debtor who responds to the letter service is yours to keep! This is quite a bargain when you consider what an attorney would charge for this same service. I especially recommend this service if your customers are spread over several states or countries.

One of the debtors on my aging was from South America. He owed $250, he was not returning my phone calls, and my letters were ignored. I was not going to spend $300 in long-distance calls and postage for a $250 debt, so I had the letter service send out its series of letters. Within three weeks, I received a check for $250 from the debtor, along with a copy of the first letter he received from the letter-writing service. Until he received that first letter, he probably had no intention of paying. The debtor knew that I would eventually stop calling him because it was too expensive, and legally I did not have much recourse. Receipt of the first collection letter obviously cast some doubt to that line of thinking.

Be familiar with the letters the collection agency sends to your clients. The letters should be firm but not threatening. They are used simply to get the attention of your clients, and you will be amazed at the attention they get. The letter service will also help you to determine if a client has no intention of paying you. Some debtors will call you immediately after receiving the first letter and offer to make payment arrangements. Obviously, they do not get many letters like this and usually are concerned about what it might do their credit. On the other hand, if a debtor is not the least bit bothered by receiving these letters, you can bet that he or she is getting many letters like this and is not even fazed by it. Odds are that the person has no intention of paying you, and this is the kind of debtor you should consider sending out for collection.

Once the collection agency has sent out its series of letters to your debtor for the agreed-upon fixed fee, its obligation ends. If you want the collection pursued further, most agencies will charge you as much as 50 percent of whatever they are able to collect. Initially, most creditors are outraged at this charge, and this is why so many collection agencies are frowned upon. However, it is up to you to be selective when you use the collection agency. Before you send the debt to a collection agency, ask yourself how much you will collect without the assistance of the collection agency. Is the answer nothing? Well, half of nothing is *nothing*. Collecting 50 percent of a receivable is still 50 percent more than you thought you would collect.

Collection agencies can be invaluable in cases of "missing" debtors. Let's say you have no idea where to locate a debtor, his or her phone number has been disconnected, and the person's mail is not being forwarded. If you have the debtor's driver's license number (it should be on the credit application), you may be able to do some skip tracing and find the person's new locale.

However, debtors who skip town to avoid their debts (and they usually have several) are usually smart enough to know how to avoid their creditors. There are courses and books on the *how to's* of skip tracing, and if you can afford to invest the time it takes to do the skip tracing, then, by all means, try to locate the person and collect your money. But I find that skip tracing is extremely time consuming and once the debtor is found, he or she is usually in another state. You must familiarize yourself with the laws of that state, and depending on the size of your business, the odds of collecting your money are slim. Even if you successfully sue the client in small claims court, the small claims court has no power to enforce payment and you are still left with the task of trying to collect on your judgment.

Small independent-owned businesses usually do not have the resources to pursue such a collection. Most collection managers have more than one debtor from whom they are trying to collect, and most of them are reachable. I would rather invest my time in collecting money from people who are within reach.

Reputable collection agencies have impressive skip tracing computer programs and can usually locate your debtor. An attorney will usually charge you for this service, while the collection agency has built this charge into its fee.

Another advantage in using a collection agency over an attorney is that in this day and age, the cost of hiring an attorney can far exceed the receivable you are trying to collect. That is exactly what the debtor is counting on, and most debtors know it is usually not cost effective to hire an attorney to collect a debt (depending on the amount due, of course).

Many debtors are experts in avoiding paying their bills and they know how to add to your attorney costs and drag out a lawsuit. However, debtors such as this are also familiar with collection agencies and how they work. The reputable collection agencies only make money when they collect the receivable and as a result, pursue it quite vigorously. Most collection agencies are connected with TRW, have strong skip tracing computer programs at their disposal, and can find assets you never knew existed. The attorney who gets paid by the hour has nothing to lose in the event your money is not recovered. The attorney will still be paid, the collection agency will not.

Admittedly, I use collection agencies for a very small percentage of my receivables, but for the times I have used them, they have been well worth the money.

Chapter 13

Attorneys

When should you stop your efforts in collecting a receivable and actually engage an attorney to sue the debtor? When you feel without a doubt that the debtor has *no* intention of paying the bill. This is very different from the debtor who cannot pay you because he or she truly has no money. Suing debtors who have no money will give you a judgment that is worthless. Or what about the debtor who is expecting a big check in one year (and has proven to you that this is true) and will pay you then. Even with a judgment, you still will not get paid until the money the person was waiting for comes in.

Nobody likes to be sued and I find it just as uncomfortable being the person on the other end. It is costly, time consuming, and aggravating, and I recommend doing whatever it takes to work out the receivable before resorting to a lawsuit.

However, there comes a time when all the "niceness" in the world will not get the debtor to pay. You have used up all your resources and have come to the end of your rope. It is now time to call in the attorney. Do not call in "any" attorney. Look around just as you did for the collection agency. Interview several and find one with whom you are comfortable.

With regard to collections, some attorneys work by the hour. However, most attorneys prefer to charge a contingent fee based on the amount of the settlement. This can range anywhere from 25 percent to 50 percent. You will also be charged for any out-of-pocket costs, such as filing fees and asset searches, because these charges are not included as part of the contingency fee.

Just as there are advantages in using a collection agency over an attorney, there are also advantages in using an attorney over a collection agency. The biggest advantage is that often you can recoup your attorney's fees from the debtor. Standard engagement letters provide for attorney's fees (see Chapter 6), and there is a good chance you will recover your debt, as well as reasonable attorney's fees and costs.

Another advantage is that the attorney hired by the collection agency may not have the expertise required to win your case. If you have a rather complicated receivable, it would be more prudent to hire your own attorney who has handled cases similar to yours. For the complicated cases, it is wise to pay attorneys on a contingency basis. Otherwise, paying them by the hour could end up costing you as much as the receivables.

It has been my experience that most debtors have no interest in going to court. Once a debtor is served with a lawsuit, he or she is put in the position of having to hire an attorney to respond to the lawsuit. This, of course, results in additional costs that the debtor cannot expect to recover. Most debtors do not think you will go so far as to sue them, and when they are actually served, they often pick up the phone and offer settlements.

It is unfortunate that it takes legal action to get the attention of a debtor, but in certain cases that is the only way in which you will get your money.

Chapter 14

Fair Debt Collection Practices Act

The best way to avoid violation of collection laws is to use common sense at all times and always remember that the debt you are calling about is nobody's business except the person who owes it. It would not make sense to call a debtor in the middle of the day if he or she works at night, unless the person has given you permission to do so. If your company just hired a new controller and he or she has a brilliant idea to send past due statements on postcards in order to save money, this person has just notified "the world" that your client does not pay bills on time. If someone tells you, "Don't ever call me again," then *don't ever call that person again.* And do not go into detail when you leave a phone message for someone. If your message was played in a court of law, did you say anything that implied that the person you called does not pay his or her bills on time? The last thing you want is to get in trouble for just doing your job.

Call the local chapter of your State Bar Association for answers to any legal questions you may have with respect to state laws. Most of the chapters have volunteer attorneys on call and you will be referred to one of them. I handle receivables in several states, so I have found this to be a great resource when I have quick questions on laws pertaining to a particular state. Also, reputable collection agencies are another great resource for you when you have legal questions (pertaining to collections). It has been my experience that reputable collection agencies are familiar with the laws in many states, and if they aren't, they can get the information in a matter of minutes. Collection agencies have been extremely helpful to me on more than one occasion.

(A note about payments: Checks dated more than six months ago are usually not cashable, no matter how much money the issuer has in the bank. The exception is U.S. Treasury checks, which are valid indefinitely. Also, if the amount written on a check in words is different from the amount written in numbers, the bank will pay the sum shown in words.)

If you receive a partial payment with the notation "paid in full," do not simply cash the check and hope to recover the balance later. The most common recommendation is to cross out "paid in full," cash the check, and send a letter to the debtors thanking them for the partial payment. If, however, the check is accompanied by a letter stating that cashing this check constitutes full and final payment, then do not cash the check unless you are will to accept it as payment in full.

As a creditor, you are also bound by the statute of limitations imposed by each state. In many states, you must file suit within four years from when the last service was performed and/or the last payment was received. At the time of this writing, oral contracts have a two-year statue of limitations in most states, while written contracts have four-year statute of limitations.

For the past four years, I have been collecting $100 a month from a debtor whose receivable dates back eight years. He has been faithful in sending these payments and, in California, the statute of limitations begins running from the date of his last payment. That is why I encourage collection managers to at least try to get a minimum payment from debtors on older receivables. If a debtor knows that the statute of limitations on his or her account is going to expire in the next few months, the person is more likely to string you along until he or she is no longer obligated by law to pay you. (By the way, debtors who do this are very familiar with the law and usually know the exact date that the statute will run). In other states, as long as you continue to send out past due statements, the statute of limitations runs four years from the last statement you sent out. Again, check with an attorney in your area if you are not clear on the laws of your state.

The Fair Debt Collection Practices Act (FDCPA) became effective in the Spring of 1978 and sets Federal guidelines for what you legally can and cannot do to collect your bills. Currently the FDCPA applies only to collection agencies and attorneys. Creditors who collect their own debts are exempt from the Act. However, it is highly encouraged that creditors comply with the provisions of the FDCPA.

The FDCPA has established the standard for determining and identifying whether an activity is an abusive collection practice, and because most state laws prohibit "abusive or unconscionable collection practices," creditors as well as collection agencies and attorneys are subject to these state laws. In fact, the FDCPA is used by the court to determine whether you have used abusive collection methods to collect your debt. So it is important to be familiar with what is considered a deceptive or abusive collection practice.

The following is an abstract of the FDCPA:

Collectors Covered by Act:

Any person, other than the creditor, who regularly collects debts owed to others. This includes attorneys who collect debts on a regular basis.

Communication

With the consumer:

A debt collector may *not* communicate with a consumer in connection with the collection of a debt without prior consent of the consumer given directly to the debt collector or the express permission of the court competent jurisdiction,

- At any unusual place or time that would be considered to be inconvenient to consumer. This inconvenient time is generally between 9 p.m. and 8 a.m.
- If the collector knows the consumer is represented by an attorney.

- At the consumer's place of employment if the debt collector knows or has reason to know that the consumer's employer prohibits the consumer from receiving such communications.

With third parties:

Generally prohibited in the absence of prior consent of the consumer given directly to the debt collector, or the express permission of the court, or as reasonably necessary to effectuate a postjudgment judicial remedy.

Ceasing Communication

The debt collector may not communicate further with the consumer if that consumer refuses to pay the debt or wishes the debt collection to cease further communication, except:

- To advise the consumer that debt collection efforts are being terminated.
- To notify the consumer that specific remedies will be undertaken.

Harassment or Abuse

The following actions are prohibited by a debt collector:

- The use of threat or use of violence or other criminal means to harm the physical person, reputation, or property of that person.
- The use of obscene or profane language that is intended to abuse the consumer.
- The publication of a list of consumers who allegedly refuse to pay debt, except to a credit reporting agency.
- The advertising for sale of any debt to coerce payment of the debt.
- Causing a telephone to ring or engaging a person in telephone conversation repeatedly with intent to annoy, abuse, or harass any person at the above number.
- The placing of telephone calls without meaningful disclosure of the caller's identity, except to locate the consumer.

False or Misleading Representations

A debt collector may not use any false, deceptive, or misleading representations as a method of collecting on any debt. The following are examples of false representations:

- Debt collector is affiliated with government agency.
- Misstating the character, amount, or legal status of any debt.
- Debt collector is an attorney.
- Nonpayment will result in arrest or imprisonment or seizure, garnishment, attachment, or sale of any property unless such actions taken are lawful and the debt collector intends to take such actions.
- The consumer committed a crime or other conduct with the intent of harming that consumer.
- Communicating or threatening to communicate false credit information that is known to be false, including failure to communicate the fact that a debt is disputed.
- Distribution of false documents.
- The use of any business, company, or other organization name other than the true name of the debt collection business, company, or organization.

Unfair Practices

Debt collectors may not use unfair or unconscionable means to collect debts. The following are examples:

- The collection of any amount (including principal, interest, or other fees) unless such amounts are expressly authorized by the agreement creating the debt or permitted by law.
- The solicitation or acceptance of a postdated check or other payment instrument postdated more than five days, unless consumer is notified in writing that collector intends to deposit check between three and 10 days prior to such deposit.
- Depositing or threatening to deposit any postdated check or other instrument prior to the date on such check or instrument.

- Causing charges (including collect phone calls) by concealing the true purpose of such communication.
- Taking or threatening to take action to effect dispossession or disablement of property if the collector does not have the right or the intent or if the property is exempt by law.
- Using a postcard to communicate with a consumer regarding a debt.
- Disguising the debt collector's business name and address on the mailing envelope.

Validation of Debt

Notice of Debt Contents

A debt collector shall furnish the consumer, within five days after initial communication, the following:

- The amount of the debt.
- The creditor to whom the debt is owed.
- A statement that unless the consumer, within 30 days after receipt of the notice, disputes the validity of the debt, the debt will be assumed valid by the collector.
- A statement that the collector will mail a copy of the verification of the debt or judgment to the consumer if that consumer requests this information within 30 days.

Disputed Debts

If the consumer disputes the debt by written notification to the debt collector within 30 days, the debt collector is required to cease collection of the debt.

Admission of Liability

The failure of a consumer to dispute the validity of the debt may not be construed by any court as an admission of the liability by that consumer.

Multiple Debts

If the consumer owes on multiple debts and makes payment on any single debt, debt collector may not apply payment to disputed debt.

Civil Liability

Amount of Damages

Except as otherwise provided, a debt collector who fails to comply with the provisions of the FDCPA with respect to any person is liable to such person an amount equal to the sum of:

- Any actual damages sustained as a result of the failure.
- Such additional damages that the court may allow, but not exceeding $1,000.
- In the event of a class action, not to exceed $500,000 or 1 percent of the net worth of the debt collector.
- Costs of the legal action, together with reasonable attorney's fees allowed by the court.

In determining the amount of damages, the court will consider the frequency and persistence of noncompliance.

The action may be brought in any United States District Court without regard to the amount in controversy, or in any other court of competent jurisdiction within one year from the date the violation occurred.

Administrative Enforcement

All of the functions and powers of the Federal Trade Commission are available to enforce compliance with the Act.

Relation to State Laws

The FDCPA does not affect or except any person from complying with the laws of any state with respect to debt collection practices except to the extent that these laws are inconsistent with any provisions of the FDCPA, and then only to the extent of the inconsistency.

A state law is not inconsistent with the Act if it allows greater consumer protection.

Chapter 15

Conclusion

Collections can be challenging and fun or grueling and tedious. Like any job, it is whatever you create it to be. The success of a company can improve dramatically when the sales and accounts receivable departments work in harmony. For this reason, when I give training seminars in companies, I encourage them to invite their sales managers to attend along with the accounts receivable department so they can gain a better understanding of what is involved in the collection process.

Suggest that your company hold weekly (or monthly) meetings that bring the sales and accounts receivable departments together. It is amazing how much you can accomplish when the lines of communication open up. But remember, you are one person and can only do what you can do. Depending on the size of the company you work for, you can only go so far. Do not become frustrated if you hit a few brick walls, and never give up on trying to make things better. Miracles do happen.

Be flexible. I have taken courses where it was stressed that a successful collections person should not have to call clients and remind them to send their monthly checks. I disagree. My philosophy is that a successful collections person collects money *period*. Do whatever it takes to get your money (in the legal and moral sense, of course).

The reality is that you are dealing with human beings, not robots. What an ideal world this would be if we could train everyone to pay their bills on time, to keep all their commitments, and to be true to their word. But this is the real world we live in and we have to learn to adapt to real people, because rarely will they adapt to us. If a debtor requires a monthly reminder call in order for you to get paid, then make the call. If a client requests a second copy of an outstanding invoice, then send it. Time consuming? Yes. Frustrating? Yes. But you will also get your money.

It is important to keep a positive attitude about people and see the good in them. You are not in the right business if you have the attitude that people who do not pay timely are less than human. This is not to say that these people do not exist. Unfortunately, there are people out there who will take advantage of anyone and anything—debtors who are so full of hot air that if you stuck a pin in them they would fly right to the moon. But it has been my experience that these types of people are few and far between.

Most of the debtors you are calling are people just like you with families depending on them and a list of obligations. Many have payrolls to meet and not only have their own families to support, but the families of all their employees depend on them, as well. Given the economy today, many are under tremendous pressure just to stay afloat. You must be sensitive to these pressures and truly have respect for the debtors who are doing everything they can to remain in business and meet their obligations. The phrase "you can catch more bees with honey" is certainly true in collections. If you cannot get the money by being nice (but firm), you definitely will not get it being mean.

Know when to give up on a collection by recognizing "sooner than later" when someone has no intention of paying you, send it out for collection, and *let it go*. Do not take it personally. You cannot win them all, but you can certainly win most! Do not criticize, condemn, or judge the debtor. Even on your worst days, it is still better to be the creditor than the debtor. Be enthusiastic in your job and see each debtor as a challenge, not as a problem. You will find that if you are willing to work with debtors, most debtors will work with you.

Periodically take seminars on collections. It is interesting to hear another collector's perspective on the world of collections. In addition, you will have a chance to interact with other collection managers and hear their "horror" stories and how they handle the various excuses they hear every day. Maybe they have a strategy that you have not tried yet and vice versa.

Remember that customers tend to pay suppliers they need and ignore those they can survive without. One example is the patient who goes to the dentist and is in severe pain. It is amazing how quickly he or she will come up with the money if the dentist demands payment in advance of the work. However, the dentist who waits until after the work is performed to collect the bill may be stuck with a past due receivable until the patient's next crisis. After all, once the root canal is finished and the pain is gone, paying for dental services is no longer a priority.

Another example is the accountant who has a receivable for a tax return. If the client suddenly becomes audited by the Internal Revenue Service and comes crying to the accountant, it is amazing how this person "suddenly" comes up with the money owed for his or her tax return, as well as the fee for the upcoming audit.

To the contractor who has been commissioned to remodel a house, do not wait until you finish remodeling the entire house before you collect your money. Collect your money upon completion of each phase. You see, most collections are just common sense. When the customer needs you, you are in a position to collect your money!

Timing is essential. The longer you wait to follow up on a bill, the harder it will be to collect. Do not put yourself in the position whereby you have waited so long to follow up on your receivables that it becomes necessary to litigate in order to collect your fees. Be consistent, persistent, efficient, and stay challenged. Give thanks for your job and turn it into a positive one. Your efforts will pay off as you collect your money and learn to work with people under extraordinary circumstances.

As a collector, you can make a difference in people's lives. I believe life is about people, not things, and that we are put in this world to learn to work with each other. Learn to work with your debtor and you will find that the rewards will be far greater than the money you *will* be collecting!

For information about lectures/seminars given by Ms. Frischer, please write or call:

CSA Publishing
Post Office Box 3685
Chatsworth, California 91313-3685
(310) 442-5364

Index